KN

THE DELECTABLE YOU:

From Aries, energy personified, to dreamy Pisces—keys to recognizing your tastiest, most tempting charms.

THE DANGEROUS YOU:

Lions can bite and Scorpions sometimes sting. Are you warm to his touch or too hot to handle?

THE SENSUOUS YOU:

Gemini girl, Libra lady, what turns you on . . . and off?

THE SECRETIVE YOU:

No-nonsense Virgo and off-beat Aquarian, who are you *really*, deep inside?

THE BEDSIDE ASTROLOGER COMPANION

THE BEDSIDE ASTROLOGER COMPANION

FRANCESCA STUART

COSMOPOLITAN

THE BEDSIDE ASTROLOGER COMPANION is an original publication of Cosmopolitan Books. This work has never before appeared in book form.

COSMOPOLITAN BOOKS
AVON BOOKS
A division of
The Hearst Corporation
1350 Avenue of the Americas
New York, New York 10019

First Cosmopolitan Books Printing: December 1995

COSMOPOLITAN TRADEMARK REG. U.S. PAT. OFF. AND IN OTHER COUNTRIES, MARCA REGISTRADA, HECHO EN U.S.A.

Printed in the U.S.A.

RA   10   9   8   7   6   5   4   3   2   1

contents

Introduction   1

Celebrity Fantasy Men   4

ARIES   March 21–April 20   5
   Aries Females of Fame and Fortune   5
   Your Special Sun Sign Attributes   6-7
   The Positive You ... The Negative
   You ... Your Hopes and Wishes ... Your
   Fears ... Your Strengths ... Your Success
   Style ... Your Money Style ... Your Health
   Style ... Your Love Style ... What Turns
   You On ... What Turns You Off   7-14
   Your Cosmic Compatibility Guide   14-19
   Most Marvelous Cosmic Matches ...
   Most Difficult Cosmic Matches   20

TAURUS   April 21–May 21   21
    Taurus Females of Fame and Fortune   21
    Your Special Sun Sign Attributes   22-23
    The Positive You . . . The Negative
    You . . . Your Hopes and Wishes . . . Your
    Fears . . . Your Strengths . . . Your Success
    Style . . . Your Money Style . . . Your Health
    Style . . . Your Love Style . . . What Turns
    You On . . . What Turns You Off   23-31
    Your Cosmic Compatibility Guide   31-36
    Most Marvelous Cosmic Matches . . .
    Most Difficult Cosmic Matches   37

GEMINI   May 22–June 21   39
    Gemini Females of Fame and Fortune   39
    Your Special Sun Sign Attributes   40-41
    The Positive You . . . The Negative
    You . . . Your Hopes and Wishes . . . Your
    Fears . . . Your Strengths . . . Your Success
    Style . . . Your Money Style . . . Your Health
    Style . . . Your Love Style . . . What Turns
    You On . . . What Turns You Off   41-50
    Your Cosmic Compatibility Guide   50-55
    Most Marvelous Cosmic Matches . . .
    Most Difficult Cosmic Matches   56

CANCER   June 22–July 23   57
    Cancer Females of Fame and Fortune   57
    Your Special Sun Sign Attributes   58-59
    The Positive You . . . The Negative
    You . . . Your Hopes and Wishes . . . Your
    Fears . . . Your Strengths . . . Your Success

Style . . . Your Money Style . . . Your Health
Style . . . Your Love Style . . . What Turns
You On . . . What Turns You Off   59-66
Your Cosmic Compatibility Guide   66-70
Most Marvelous Cosmic Matches . . .
Most Difficult Cosmic Matches   71

LEO   July 24–August 23   73
Leo Females of Fame and Fortune   73
Your Special Sun Sign Attributes   74-75
The Positive You . . . The Negative
You . . . Your Hopes and Wishes . . . Your
Fears . . . Your Strengths . . . Your Success
Style . . . Your Money Style . . . Your Health
Style . . . Your Love Style . . . What Turns
You On . . . What Turns You Off   75-82
Your Cosmic Compatibility Guide   83-87
Most Marvelous Cosmic Matches . . .
Most Difficult Cosmic Matches   88

VIRGO   August 24–September 23   89
Virgo Females of Fame and Fortune   89
Your Special Sun Sign Attributes   90-91
The Positive You . . . The Negative
You . . . Your Hopes and Wishes . . . Your
Fears . . . Your Strengths . . . Your Success
Style . . . Your Money Style . . . Your Health
Style . . . Your Love Style . . . What Turns
You On . . . What Turns You Off   91-99
Your Cosmic Compatibility Guide   99-104
Most Marvelous Cosmic Matches . . .
Most Difficult Cosmic Matches   105

LIBRA   September 24–October 23   107
  Libra Females of Fame and Fortune   107
  Your Special Sun Sign Attributes   108-109
  The Positive You . . . The Negative
  You . . . Your Hopes and Wishes . . . Your
  Fears . . . Your Strengths . . . Your Success
  Style . . . Your Money Style . . . Your Health
  Style . . . Your Love Style . . . What Turns
  You On . . . What Turns You Off   109-116
  Your Cosmic Compatibility Guide   116-121
  Most Marvelous Cosmic Matches . . .
  Most Difficult Cosmic Matches   122

SCORPIO   October 24–November 22   123
  Scorpio Females of Fame and Fortune   123
  Your Special Sun Sign Attributes   124-125
  The Positive You . . . The Negative
  You . . . Your Hopes and Wishes . . . Your
  Fears . . . Your Strengths . . . Your Success
  Style . . . Your Money Style . . . Your Health
  Style . . . Your Love Style . . . What Turns
  You On . . . What Turns You Off   125-133
  Your Cosmic Compatibility Guide   133-137
  Most Marvelous Cosmic Matches . . .
  Most Difficult Cosmic Matches   138

SAGITTARIUS   November 23–December 21   139
  Sagittarius Females of Fame and Fortune   139
  Your Special Sun Sign Attributes   140-141
  The Positive You . . . The Negative
  You . . . Your Hopes and Wishes . . . Your
  Fears . . . Your Strengths . . . Your Success

Style . . . Your Money Style . . . Your Health
Style . . . Your Love Style . . . What Turns
You On . . . What Turns You Off   141-149
Your Cosmic Compatibility Guide   149-154
Most Marvelous Cosmic Matches . . .
Most Difficult Cosmic Matches   155

CAPRICORN   December 22–January 20   157
Capricorn Females of Fame and Fortune   157
Your Special Sun Sign Attributes   158-159
The Positive You . . . The Negative
You . . . Your Hopes and Wishes . . . Your
Fears . . . Your Strengths . . . Your Success
Style . . . Your Money Style . . . Your Health
Style . . . Your Love Style . . . What Turns
You On . . . What Turns You Off   159-167
Your Cosmic Compatibility Guide   167-172
Most Marvelous Cosmic Matches . . .
Most Difficult Cosmic Matches   173

AQUARIUS   January 21–February 19   175
Aquarius Females of Fame and Fortune   175
Your Special Sun Sign Attributes   176-177
The Positive You . . . The Negative
You . . . Your Hopes and Wishes . . . Your
Fears . . . Your Strengths . . . Your Success
Style . . . Your Money Style . . . Your Health
Style . . . Your Love Style . . . What Turns
You On . . . What Turns You Off   177-185
Your Cosmic Compatibility Guide   185-190
Most Marvelous Cosmic Matches . . .
Most Difficult Cosmic Matches   191

PISCES   **February 20–March 20**   *193*
   Pisces Females of Fame and Fortune   *193*
   Your Special Sun Sign Attributes   *194-195*
   The Positive You . . . The Negative
   You . . . Your Hopes and Wishes . . . Your
   Fears . . . Your Strengths . . . Your Success
   Style . . . Your Money Style . . . Your Health
   Style . . . Your Love Style . . . What Turns
   You On . . . What Turns You Off   *195-203*
   Your Cosmic Compatibility Guide   *203-207*
   Most Marvelous Cosmic Matches . . .
   Most Difficult Cosmic Matches   *208*

Conclusion   *209*

introduction

Dear girls, here it is, THE BEDSIDE ASTROL-OGER COMPANION, *new and expanded!* This year's personal, in-depth guide to your *unique* personality has *three times more* categories than last year's. It covers all the fascinating facets of your character so that you can read scads and scads about *you*—and HIM too, of course!

The information you find on the following pages puts you ahead of the stars! Why leave *anything* to chance or fate when you can look it up and have *all* the answers before you? Every-one knows that a girl who is *very* aware is not only ahead of the game, she *runs* it! With THE BEDSIDE ASTROLOGER COMPANION putting the inside info about yourself *and* him at your very fingertips, you too can be on top! What fun!

For instance, you meet a guy who's pretty cute but you're really not sure. So should you? Look him up!

Or, you've fallen madly in love and you want to know if it will last a lifetime. What are the chances *really*? Look it up!

Or, there is trouble in what seemed to be paradise and you *want* to rationalize what he's doing but *will it do you in*? Look it up!

THE BEDSIDE ASTROLOGER COMPANION *tells all*. Trust it! It's better than your best friend, because, let's face it, without THE BEDSIDE ASTROLOGER COMPANION she's in the dark just as much as you are. So get with it and find out:

- Everything about you that you *need* to know!
- How wonderful you can be!
- The areas in which you could be better—for your own sake!
- Those special sexy qualities that make him surrender!

AND NEW THIS YEAR:

- Your strengths!
- Your success style!
- Your money style!
- Your health style!
- Your love style!

Of course, THE BEDSIDE ASTROLOGER COMPANION also goes into WHAT MEN ADORE ABOUT YOU and YOUR PERSONAL POWER! In this book *you* are important, not just him. After all, if you don't show him how important you are, why should he be impressed? *You* have to impress him, dear girl, and *you* have to decide whether he's even worth the bother.

You'll also get the lowdown on your *unique*:

- Astro Symbol
- Ruling Planet
- Essential Element
- Primal Passion
- Magic Color
- Magic Jewel
- Lucky Day
- Magic Number
- Special Body Part
- Astro Flower
- and What You Have to Learn!

For fun, there's a list of the rich and famous females born in your sign as well as the sexiest male celeb for each sign of the zodiac. In addition, this year's *expanded* compatibility guide lets you *immediately* look up any man you meet and see how he gets along with your sign!

In these pages there is everything you need to know—*and* a little more, for fun! So have fun, dear girl—and get *smart* about your stars too!

CELEBRITY FANTASY MEN

ARIES
Alec Baldwin

TAURUS
Emilio Estevez

GEMINI
Johnny Depp

CANCER
Tom Cruise

LEO
Mick Jagger

VIRGO
Richard Gere

LIBRA
Sting

SCORPIO
Harry Hamlin

SAGITTARIUS
John Kennedy, Jr.

CAPRICORN
Mel Gibson

AQUARIUS
Matt Dillon

PISCES
Bruce Willis

aries
march 21 – april 20

Jessica Lange

Ali MacGraw

Diana Ross

Sarah Jessica Parker

Gloria Steinem

Erica Jong

Aretha Franklin

Here is your sun sign's most significant information, which includes everything from your ruling planet (every sign has a planet that rules it), the element of your sun sign—whether it is fire (inspirational), air (cerebral), earth (practi-

cal), or water (emotional)—to what color, jewel, and day of the week are uniquely you. It even includes your personal power, what men adore about you, and what you have to learn!

YOUR SPECIAL SUN SIGN ATTRIBUTES

Symbol:
The ram

Ruling Planet:
Mars

Essential Element:
fire

Primal Passion:
recognition

Magic Color:
red

Magic Jewel:
diamond

Lucky Day:
Sunday

Magic Number:
5

Body Part:
head

Flower:
honeysuckle

Your Personal Power:
initiation

What You Have to Learn:
patience

What Men Adore About You:
your heat

The Positive You

Energy personified, you are like a light in a deep, dark forest. The Aries girl precedes herself! You are the queen of initiation, supercharged with confidence and enthusiasm. You start projects others shy away from, and complete them while everyone else is in the beginning stage. Fiercely ambitious, fueled by ideas and fired by the need to get things going quickly, you are a leader equal to any task and a great motivator. Fully alive, fearless and eager to do so many things at once, you move at the pace of lightning, dazzling your fans and evoking sheer dread in your enemies!

Ever impatient for what's to come, you are like a wide-eyed child at Christmas plunging joyously into life. Adventurous and headstrong, you make things happen. Martian girl, you have the power to create everything you need! Sit around and wait? Complain? Not a chance. You take charge and make a bad situation better.

You're a perpetual motion machine, an eternal fountain of energy. Everyone is impressed with how much you accomplish—and in so little time too! Your zest for living is contagious and puts others in a better mind frame.

There's no ambiguity with you and very little second-guessing. You let everyone know where you stand. You make up your mind in record time and never waste an opportunity through silly hesitation. You also *create* your own opportunities! The Aries girl can turn lead to gold and get everyone to buy it!

A great head for *creating* a business, you instinctively know how to start it all up and get others to do the dirty work. Having no patience whatsoever with obstacles, Aries girl, you never *see* them—or else they crumble in your path. And since you can't stand the idea of being in second place, you will drive yourself to the top—and own it! Impulsive, spontaneous and self motivated, you are a dauntless, dynamic, trailblazer who is best off being boss and who always needs new challenges. Moving straight and fast on your course and never acknowledging opposition, you are the highest of the superachievers, a light unto yourself, a one-woman organization.

Warm, passionate and emotional, you are a fierce friend in need and an instantaneous heroine in a crisis. A girl who's ridiculously popular, you have a million friends and as many lovers as you have time for. Men are putty in your presence, dear girl, and usually want more of you than you want to give. (After all, there is so much on your plate at any given moment!) They also have to *earn* attention from this femme fatale. You don't come cheaply or easily—and there are so many others in line!

The Negative You

Fiery girl, take care not to burn the candle at both ends and burn yourself out. Too much too soon can be a bad thing. Excessive impatience *can* breed discontent. It can also burn those poor souls around you who stand too close to your flame.

Dear girl, you *can* be a bit *too* self-centered at times. So, remember that others have *their* needs too. Acting without thinking can bruise those who get in your way. And seeing yourself as the very *center* of the universe can be terribly boring for conversation.

You can be something of an *enfant terrible* when you don't get your way. And the silly thing is that you think you *always* should. You're a trifle insensitive at times. And you don't hear terribly well when the conversation doesn't revolve around you. When your sentences all begin with "I" and end with "me" it is time to back off and give others *their* time—especially if you want to have friends.

Dear girl, you're sometimes a little too pushy and impatient. People don't need to be pummeled—there are other ways to get their attention. Jealous, competitive, and at times a little cruel, you have the kind of candor that can kill.

Watch your sharp tongue, girl, or one day you may find a knife in your back.

At your worst, Aries girl, you're a narcissist with no understanding of the word "no." You need to grow up and get beyond yourself—or else you will end up all by yourself. When your desire for attention far exceeds your ability to listen, you have to ask yourself what's wrong, girl. And the answer is you!

Your Hopes and Wishes

You want it *all*, the faster the better, the more, the more divine. Your *greatest* wish is to have *everything* go your way every day of your life. Success, power, money, and status are at the top of your list. But you also want a grand love, someone glamorous and never boring. You long to be excited, dazzled, enthralled, entertained, and amused. You adore being thought of in a highly flattering way, of course. You love flash and dazzle, people who are exciting and men who make you feel like never in their entire life have they seen someone so stunning.

Your Fears

The most fearless sign of the zodiac, you don't stop long enough to even see the things that normally cause panic. However, under your intrepid persona is a little girl who needs a lot of love. All your fears and anxieties come from not feeling *enough* validation—thus, your constant need for attention. Because you sometimes move too fast to feel real, you need others to affirm you and fill you with love.

Your Strengths

Yours is the strongest, most courageous sign of the zodiac, the sign of the warrior, the conqueror, the heroine goddess. However, the most luminous thing about you is your energy and enthusiasm. You are a walking magnetic force field that dazzles people and draws them to you.

Positive, assertive, and usually on the mark, you make successes out of others' failures and light the way for more to come. You are a hard working, forward thinking, no nonsense accomplishmentarian, who is super smart, very savvy, and ahead of her time. You can make magic with your will. You take charge with true authority. Once you show up, everything simply snaps into place.

Vibrant and tons of fun to be around, you're an exciting friend to have, Aries girl. You get things going fast and know where to take them!

Your Success Style

Totally motivated and determined to be number one, you are the personification of power. You charge ahead where goddesses fear to tread, allowing nothing to deter you. Because you are such a self-starter, you can work for yourself or be an entrepreneur who takes on many different kinds of projects. Loving challenge like you love the wind in your face, you thrive on new enterprises that take your total attention.

You formulate your goals early on and can keep them in sight through the middle of a major crisis. A natural leader with an intuitive sense of organization, you like to lay the groundwork, dictate what has to be done, and have your worker bees take it from there. Your vision and leadership qualities are so outstanding you can shine in the most competitive professions. Being a movie producer or director, president of a corporation or the entire country isn't out of the question for the innovative, ambitious Aries girl. You're so dynamic, creative and highly capable, that whatever you do, your success is assured.

Your Money Style

Your impetuous, impulsive nature can lead to serious spending problems. When you see an object you love at first sight, you have to have it, and your substantially profligate ways can put you in some tense situations. Although your ability to make money is extraordinary, so is your ability to go through it. You love to power dress. You love luxury items. They are symbols of your self-worth. They make you feel so very, very shiny. And why should you save for a rainy day, anyway? It's so boring (and clouds are only for other people)!

Your Health Style

Aries girl, no one has to tell you to get in touch with your body. You see the importance of doing what's best for it. Naturally athletic and energetic, you love to exercise, and you do it regularly. Vain and proud of your sexual attractiveness, you watch *what* you eat and make sure not to eat too much. Calorie counting and scale watching is second nature to you, although you do have a special fondness for champagne and tequila.

Your Love Style

Fiery, romantic and very sexual, your restless nature finds release in passion. You can fall in love in ten minutes and out of love in five. There has to be enough excitement to initially entice you and enough hot sex to keep you interested. You love love, maybe more than anything else. And you manage to find it in a lot of places. Passionate love affairs are your favorite way to create drama, and in the spirit of the adventure, you sometimes forget that there's someone waiting for you at home. Hot romance makes everything larger than life. It all comes together—and off you go! When caught in the thralls, nothing else matters. Once again, you're reborn in bed— if only for the moment.

What Turns You On

Men who are as hot and wild as you are! You love men who are strong and sexually assertive, romantic and willing to do *anything* fun that comes to mind. You also like your men *successful* and generous. Roses every day enhance your sexual imagination, and expensive little gifts go straight to your heart. Overall, the more larger-than-life he is *in every way*, the more you're turned on and momentarily taken by him.

What Turns You Off

Weak, colorless men—the kind you can only describe as *nice*—make you turn the other way. You cannot be bothered with men who are boring or petty or whiny or those who simply seem to have no vision. Men who are bad in bed need not even call you a second time. And men who are *cheap* are simple-minded fools to think that you would even sit through dinner!

Your Cosmic Compatibility Guide

Note: This shows you how someone with your sun sign is most likely to get along with someone with his sun sign. Some combinations are instant chemistry; some are more challenging and require work and patience on both your parts. Keep in mind that this is based only on the sun sign. There are ten planets in all, and in a complete horoscope they are all important influences that affect the life of the relationship.

Aries: This is a forest fire that lights up the sky. The two of you are wicked and always *ready*! On first meeting you blast into space like a major satellite launching. Here is your romantic, passionate, wild-spirited equal! After being blinded by the light, you have eyes for no one but each other. You may also forget to eat, where you're going, what time it is. But, so what? Isn't it fun!?

Taurus: In bed he's your match, but out of bed he *can* be boring. His daily rhythm is slow, while you burn up your wires being *fast*. You crave constant excitement. He's content in front of the TV. You are impatient and intuitive. He is terribly patient and a little thick. He's a slave to his routines. You hate to do the same thing twice. You need novelty; he thrives on repetition. You need challenges; he wants bastions of security. Surely, this is not a flame that will *stay* in your heart.

Gemini: You will soon become infatuated with this quicksilver fellow. He is so clever and amusing that he kindles your fire. He's so smart and restless that he challenges *your* smarts. He is galvanized by your incandescent enthusiasm. You are arrested by his zany sense of humor. He makes you laugh at yourself. You make him glad to be alive. Together you are quite the dynamic duo. This could be until death do you part!

Cancer: Alas, you will scare the poor crab to death with all your fiery energy and occasional bouts of temper. He needs cuddling and cajoling, not commands. He will annoy you intensely with his moods and many emotional tirades. And as he provokes you, you'll create more. His possessiveness will try your patience to the point of putting up a wall. And when the crab finds himself out in the cold, he'll come on stronger. The more you pry him off your foot, the more this poor guy will cling. You need to plan a very clever escape if you want to free yourself of this murky fellow.

Leo: There is instantaneous chemistry between you two fire signs as each sends the other sexy signals across a crowded room. You love his style: regal and showy. He loves yours: self-confident and sexy. He will shower you with all those lustrous attentions of which you so approve—flowers in every room, plane tickets to exotic places, and, of course, some expensive little trinkets. You will keep him so happy in bed that he will be late for his chairman-of-the-board meetings (for the very first time in his ambitious life). He knows the way into your heart and you know what to do with his body. The two of you seem seamless from the start.

Virgo: You won't let this poor nitpicking fellow hang around long enough to show you just how boring he can be. You are interested in the big picture while he is lost in painstaking details.

You want to have fun. He wants to find the TV guide. You want to dine at an elegant, trendy French restaurant. He wants to have a little soup at the counter in the local diner. If someone locked you up in a room with him overnight, you might get so cranky you would use your karate. Give him a chance. Let him live.

Libra: This dashing fellow has *class*, and he's no dummy either! He's also a delight in bed and adores the way you show him how much you want to be there. Like you, he adores champagne, elegant restaurants, expensive clothes—all the finer things in life. You approve of his taste and the way he compliments you over candlelight. He approves of the way you turn him on. He is imaginative and thoughtful, romantic and, like you, very much in love with love. He is also so cool and refined that you can show him to your friends without fearing their bafflement. This could be the guy who grabs your attention for good!

Scorpio: This is SEX from the start. The two of you will disappear for days. Your relatives will report you to missing persons. Your attraction is based on primitive, instinctual stuff, not communication, spiritual bonds, or friendship. And do you care? Only on the way *to* the bedroom!

Sagittarius: He is a winsome fellow wonderful to flirt with, a playmate into all *kinds* of physical activity, and an adventurer par excellence who will invite you to do all sorts of exotic things. There *is* a little problem with his follow-through, however. For instance, when you show up at the airport, he might ask you what you're doing there. He is exuberant in the moment as any bubbly, bouncy one-year-old boy, and also acts like one. He doesn't remember all his wonderful plans. Offering these invitations for future adventures is just his way of having a good time. Now when it comes to such matters, Mars lady *must* be taken seriously. Too proud to beg or be taken lightly, you might have to give him a few "learning experiences" that he *won't* forget!

Capricorn: This sexual stallion does wonders for your libido. But he is more than a trifle bossy. You like his "look" and his Armani taste. However, so does he, and he lets you know it a little too often. He expects you to be totally impressed. He acts as if he is *your* greatest accomplishment. You can tell him that you were just awarded a Nobel prize and he probably won't hear you. He's too busy interrupting to tell you about his success. Not even your irritation can get through to him (he'll tell you that you have some sort of problem). At this point you do, and he's it. Get rid of him!

Aquarius: He could be your best friend, but a lover? Not for very long. Mr. Aquarius is very *detached*, and you are very emotional. He likes "the idea" of everything whereas you like to get down and dirty. In bed he is cheerful but far more mechanical than passionate—and to even get him there in the first place, you have to listen to all his fascinating intellectual theories. Your utter lack of patience makes this a one-time-only romantic scenario. But as a buddy he'll keep in touch and call you from time to time to discuss the curiosities of all his other girl "friends."

Pisces: You are captivated by the way he sees right through you—and keeps telling you more and more! He will write you love poems. He'll look into your eyes and tell you you're *uniquely* beautiful. (You could have written the script and had him memorize it.) Of course, you're completely in love. Then you find the same love poems addressed to someone named Sally. When confronted, Mr. Pisces will tell you he loves you *more*! But he is easily confused about who is who and to whom he gave what and whether or not he really loves anybody at all! Confusion and charm are the little boat he sails down the stream of life straight into the souls of so many women. Obviously he does not share your style of truth telling and direct confrontation. Forewarned is forearmed, my dear, and here you might need a lot of armor!

MOST MARVELOUS
COSMIC MATCHES

Aries March 21–April 20
Leo July 24–August 23
Libra September 24–October 23

MOST DIFFICULT
COSMIC MATCHES

Virgo August 24–September 23
Capricorn December 22–January 20
Cancer June 22–July 23

taurus
april 21 – may 21

TAURUS FEMALES OF FAME AND FORTUNE

Janet Jackson
Tori Spelling
Natasha Richardson
Cher
Candice Bergen
Michelle Pfeiffer
Barbra Streisand
Valerie Bertinelli
Grace Jones
Bianca Jagger
Audrey Hepburn
Shirley MacLaine

Here is your sun sign's most significant information, which includes everything from your ruling planet (every sign has a planet that rules it), the element of your sun sign—whether it is fire (inspirational), air (cerebral), earth (practical), or water (emotional)—to what color, jewel, and day of the week are uniquely you. It even includes your personal power, what men adore about you, and what you have to learn!

YOUR SPECIAL SUN SIGN ATTRIBUTES

Symbol:
The bull

Ruling Planet:
Venus

Essential Element:
earth

Primal Passion:
material security

Magic Color:
green

Magic Jewel:
Emerald

Lucky Day:
Friday

Magic Number:
6

Body Parts:
throat and neck

Flowers:
rose, poppy, foxglove

Your Personal Power:
warmth

What You Have to Learn:
intellectual openness and flexibility

What Men Adore About You:
your sensual femininity

The Positive You

A bastion of strength in an emotional storm, you are an unflappable angel who is always there for a friend in need. Your supportive personality puts you on almost everyone's list of favorite friends. You are the middle-of-the-night savior and the sensitive listener, patient and calm.

Sensuous, sensual, and serious about your creature comforts, you can make a sad little studio apartment seem sumptuous. It's all in the way you put things together—with a sensibility not only for how things look but also for how they feel. You entertain with style, elegance, and such *ease*! In the midst of a major extravaganza, you emerge completely unruffled and in control. You are a unique femme fatale who lives fully through her feminine nature, and channels her need to nurture and be nurtured into the attention she gives to her body and her home. Your clothes, your furnishings, and your overall personal maintenance program all reflect your love of physical luxury.

With Venus as your ruler, you are also a creative creature who can excell in artsy endeavors such as decorating, designing, cooking, sculpting, or singing (Taurus rules the throat). However, if you so choose, you can be a whiz in the business world as well.

Solid and centered, you're ready with a practical solution while others panic. Stable and well organized, you're able to accomplish any task you set out to do. You outlast the purely inspired and impatient because you know that it is not enough just to get the ideas. You have to follow through with the petty details too. And, dear girl, you do. While others fade out, you persevere and put all obstacles behind you.

You are an asset in a world where money talks. Your material nature and common sense set you apart as someone who can not only make money but handle it too! Whether you're appraising an antique or your own time, you have an instinct for what things are worth. And as a result, you can set boundaries with bullies. You know how to make them back off and move to your beat—which is slow and steady, surefooted and very, very firm.

Because you are uncomplicated and unassuming, you strike strangers as someone terribly familiar. However, you're actually a little standoffish, at least at first. You want to see what a new person is like and gather a number of concrete details about him before you go further. But once your earthy, practical, slightly conservative soul is satisfied and you feel fully committed, you are capable of being loyal for a lifetime and prepared to stand by a significant someone through all sorts of turmoil.

The Negative You

The difficult you tends to see things in black and white with no shades of gray in between. The nuances you overlook can hold you back, especially in the area of love. When you allow your subjectivity to blind you, you can make very bad emotional choices and then stubbornly stick to them. You tend to fall for the wrong men for the wrong reasons and hold on for dear life once you've dug in. You are especially vulnerable to looks, money, power, and prestige. You think they mean you've met a nice person. However, after it's clear to even the cleaning lady that you're not being *treated* very nicely, you still are not convinced. Worse yet, you're apt to repeat the same mistakes with the next guy you meet and the one after that. Tauruses never look within to figure out why they keep doing what they do. Instead, they look without—for another man.

The Taurus girl can be stubborn, thick, and highly judgmental of others—if the others are women, that is. She values men. She won't hesitate to cancel dinner with her best friend at the last minute if some good-looking jerk gives her a jingle.

The Taurus girl with her worst foot forward is needy, and it shows. She is also selfish, painfully insensitive, and so quick to ingratiate herself to any man she thinks has status and power that she is incapable of being a real friend to anyone, including herself. Superficial, foolhardy, and self-righteous sum up your down side, dear girl. And talk about holding a grudge! The negative Taurus girl hangs on and on to *all* the wrong things—and can't seem to see the light of how to let go.

Your Hopes and Wishes

Your greatest wish is for a relationship with a fairy tale ending. Of course, emotional and material security with all the right creature comforts is your idea of a "happy ever after" kind of life. Unless you are one of those primal Earth Mother type Taurus girls, a big bank account is top on your list of priorities. Since money makes you feel secure and cared for in an otherwise cold and insecure world, your secret fantasy is to be taken care of by a very rich man.

Children are also important in your scheme of things. Taurus girls have strong maternal instincts. Having children is your way of connecting to a part of yourself that needs continuity. Through your child, you feel more alive, more loved. And at your best, it is your own generous heart that acts as a magnet for all the love you feel you need.

Your Fears

Your deepest fear is being poor and alone. You also have a fear of being betrayed by your lover. The jealousy and possessiveness deeply embedded in your nature are based on this fear of abandonment. The Taurus girl is *not* thrilled when her man has a hoard of female friends. She has no intention of sharing him in any way. A rock solid situation with no interference from the outside is how she holds onto what she feels is hers. A Taurus girl in a jealous rage is a death goddess on a rampage.

The Taurus girl also has a fear of aging that threatens her sense of well-being. Since she would love to look like a seventeen-year-old model with no body fat for the rest of her life, it depresses her to see the signs that separate her from this fantasy. This girl considers her appearance such a source of personal power that she may not get to know and like herself.

Your Strengths

You are capable of boundless love and the sort of devotion immortalized by seventeenth-century romantic poets. You have a warmth that comforts, nurtures, supports, and heals. You are also a successful builder of ideas, things, buildings, projects, and families. You know how to plant the seed, how to harvest the crop, and what to do in between. You have a sense of beauty, color, and texture that creates comfortingly enfolding experiences. Finally, you have the patience and concentration to complete any task. When these talents are projected out into the world, the Taurus girl can raise huge amounts of money for worthy charity funds. Through her heart, on a personal level, and through her vision and efforts on a global level, she can help to change the world. Now that's power!

Your Success Style

You are a practical girl who gets what she wants through planning, organization, and perseverance. You can run someone else's business or start your own, turning either into a multi-million-dollar venture. The hardest of workers and a nitty-gritty problem solver, you set your sights on the top and keep going till you get there!

Business and financial acumen aren't *all* you have going for you! You also possess a creative ability that begs to be expressed. You could be an architect, a sculptor, an interior designer, or a landscaper. And it is commonly known that Taurus is the sign of the singer.

Your Money Style

You are *such* a clever girl with money. You know how to make it *and* how to make it work for you. Frankly, you love it—or, more precisely, the luxury and freedom it buys. You love spending to buy those things that make you feel queenly and comforted. However, it's also possible for you to be a little chintzy at times (generally the wrong ones!) or to look at cost a trifle more than you should. One of your little secrets is that you love to spend on yourself but sometimes resent having to spend on someone else: It all depends on how secure you feel that day. But whatever your personal pattern, dear Taurus girl, take care not to let money rule you. Try to remain a free agent untwisted by dollar signs.

Your Health Style

Face it, Taurus girl, exercise will never replace food on your list of pleasures. It's anything *but* a peak experience for you. Staying healthy may not be your top priority either. However, weight—or its opposite, starving yourself to compensate for all the things you would like to eat—can be a problem. Your fondness for rich foods will do you in if you don't discipline yourself. Indeed, excess of all kinds is a potential pitfall for your personality. So, naturally your favorite way to burn off calories from that double chocolate-peanut butter mousse pie is sex to excess!

Your Love Style

You are an earthy romantic who feels completely lost without a partner. The single lifestyle—waiting for the phone to ring and sleeping with your cat—is not for you. Whenever you don't have a lover, you want, need, and sometimes are utterly desperate for one. And you are willing to do a *lot* to get and keep him. The patient, giving female is a role you play with panache. You play it because you want to get married or at least nail the guy down for good. Sometimes you pay *too* high a price, though, or don't see that Mr. Right is all wrong. Being a fixed sign, you can wait indefinitely for things to change from impossible to "highly desirable." (Nicole Simpson was a Taurus.) Although strong needs for sex and security will always push you in certain directions, don't allow them to seal your fate in cement. Make sure you have a soul mate, not a cellmate, or else you will find yourself in a situation you never bargained for. And remember, when you learn to say no to the wrong relationships, you open the door for the right one to come in.

What Turns You On

You adore being touched in all the right places, and *taken* to the right places as well. All the traditional romantic trappings *get* your attention, but it's what happens between the sheets that keeps it. You want a man who wants to stay in bed for days. Ideally, he'll also be handsome, rich, powerful, and fond of giving gifts. It will do if he is simply hot, though. Hot *and* handsome will make you fall in love. Hot, handsome, and rich will make you fall *madly* in love. And of course, a big diamond is one of the biggest turnons of all.

What Turns You Off

Any man who flaunts another woman in your face might as well be dead. The first hint that he's a roving-eyed, smooth-talking playboy puts you in a very cool and distant place. Signs of a potential cheat affect you like a red flag waved in front of a bull. And you'd *never* give your real phone number to someone whose initial presentation is crude, rude, or uncool. You are a Venus-ruled girl, after all, and need to feel attracted to a man's total appearance. If that doesn't grab you, he won't.

Your Cosmic Compatibility Guide

Note: This shows you how someone with your sun sign is most likely to get along with someone with his sun sign. Some combinations are instant chemistry; some are more challenging and require work and patience on both your parts. Keep in mind that this is based only on the sun sign. There are ten planets in all, and in a complete horoscope they are all important influences that affect the life of the relationship.

Aries: He is sexy, self-confident and full of energy. He will overwhelm you with his passion and put you in a realm of the senses that sends you reeling. Ardent, romantic, and impulsive, in the heat of the moment he will do something so sublime that you hear wedding bells. But beware, dear Taurus girl, this man is something of a fly-by-night. He also lives by a basic rule: *his* interests *are* the rule. Don't let yourself be heartbroken. Take it slow.

Taurus: Like you, he is sensual, earthy, and dependable. He is also secure financially. While you tend to go and get yourself heartbroken by the "bad boys," this fellow will make you feel worthy and cared for. The two of you may start to fall into routines that get a little moldy, but that can be dealt with down the road. In the meantime, he is the kind of guy who wants what you want—and what could be better?

Gemini: This type of fellow needs a challenge to keep his attention focused. *You* need to know where you stand at all costs. You hate games. He loves them. His mercurial, restless nature is more suited to women with the same rhythm. He *is* a good lover, but only in the moment. So don't expect it to last.

Cancer: While Taurus girl-Cancer guy is a common combo, he is not as sweet as he may look on first sight. He is also complicated, moody, utterly subjective—and will expect *you* to accommodate his craziness. You probably will. You will read his possessiveness as proof of his fidelity, but it's not. It's his insecurity. Mr. Cancer *is* capable of being unfaithful, but he'll torture you if he even suspects you of the same. Sometimes there is no reasoning with this man. He hears only his own thoughts. It doesn't matter if you tell him that your hair is on fire. He won't get it.

Leo: Ah yes, he is sure to get your attention with his dash and dazzle and terribly high opinion of himself. How can you resist all those romantic dinners, even if the conversation is all about him? Well, you can't. You want more. You get it. He comes with flowers, maybe a few trinkets, too. This man is a flirt, though. He can't resist a pretty face, especially if it seems to be smiling for him only. (And with his ego, he's sure they all are.) This man is great for entertainment, but beware, the show could turn out to be a carnival.

Virgo: Now here is a fellow who will take you seriously. Yes, he is a bit predictable, reluctant to break out of his routines and maybe a tad *too* cautious. But he is also a sensitive, earthy lover who won't disappoint you. You have the patience for his painstaking approach to life. (Not everyone has.) In turn, you get a caring person you can count on and a shared life to look forward to down the road.

Libra: He is a charmer capable of stealing your heart. Mr. Libra is smooth. He is a sensual lover, sensitive to all the romantic touches that make an evening magic. However, he is emotionally cool, superficial, and a flirt, a real fool for a beautiful body. Beauty is his religion. Fun-filled and amusing, yes, but don't count on him completely. While fabulous in the moment, Mr. Libra is a fickle fellow who might forget your first name should he find himself in a compromising situation.

Scorpio: This fellow is a fatal attraction—sexy, magnetic, mysterious, passionate, and *dangerous*! To say the least, Mr. Scorpio is never up-front about anything. To say more, he's controlling, manipulative, and very tricky. There is *always* more to him than meets the eye. Maybe even a wife. He likes his little games. He'll always play them. His mind twists and turns, while yours is a straight arrow. Take heed and proceed with caution.

Sagittarius: This footloose, fancy-free chap is so forgetful he could stand you up at the airport. Mr. Sag. is an adventurer, always dashing about doing something that he thinks is terribly important. Saving the rain forests one day, taking an impromptu trip to Tibet to climb a glacier the next. His is the sign of travel and higher philosophies. Yours is the sign of solid earthly foundations. You want to plan your future. He's a truly serendipitous sort who only wants to plan where he'll go next. Needless to say, you mix like oil and water. There's no chemistry, and such a basic communication problem that it will be a miracle if you can even hear each other. Nice try, but no diamond ring.

Capricorn: This serious fellow knows exactly where he's going (and how much money he's going to make each step of the way). He is materialism personified, a man who will buy you diamonds, build you a house, and be a proper father. He'll also play father to *you*—his favorite thing is telling people what to do. You won't really mind, though. The Goat is tireless in bed and the best provider of the zodiac. What more could you ask for?

Aquarius: He is a supercerebral loner who seems to be from another universe. Emotionally remote and impractical yet full of ideas, Mr. Aquarius would rather talk all night or play with his computer than make love. He will put you to sleep explaining cybernetics—and then slip quietly out the door. And that just *won't* do. This guy needs to date through the e-mail. *You* need someone to hug.

Pisces: This sensual, intuitive, seductive fellow can make you fall in love overnight. He will make love to you till dawn, tell you that he loves you, and you'll soon feel he's your cherished soul mate. Could this be a fantasy come true? Perhaps. The trouble is that the Neptune man's mind is *full* of fantasies—and many of them are about women. There's a reason his astrological symbol is two fish swimming in different directions. This man's mind is going so many different ways at once and his emotions are so changeable that you cannot expect consistency from him. Best advice: don't go by what he says. Watch what he does.

MOST MARVELOUS
COSMIC MATCHES

Capricorn December 22–January 20
Taurus April 21–May 21
Aries March 21–April 20

MOST DIFFICULT
COSMIC MATCHES

Pisces February 20–March 20
Scorpio October 24–November 22
Gemini May 22–June 21

gemini
may 22 – june 21

GEMINI FEMALES OF FAME AND FORTUNE

Annette Bening

Paula Abdul

Brooke Shields

Kathleen Turner

Priscilla Presley

Cyndi Lauper

Joan Collins

Isabella Rossellini

Marilyn Monroe

Wynonna Judd

Sandra Bernhard

Here is your sun sign's most significant information, which includes everything from your ruling planet (every sign has a planet that rules it), the element of your sun sign—whether it is fire (inspirational), air (cerebral), earth (practical), or water (emotional)—to what color, jewel, and day of the week are uniquely you. It even includes your personal power, what men adore about you, and what you have to learn!

YOUR SPECIAL SUN SIGN ATTRIBUTES

Symbol:
The twins

Ruling Planet:
Mercury

Essential Element:
air

Primal Passion:
connection

Magic Color:
yellow

Magic Jewel:
aquamarine

Lucky Day:
Wednesday

Magic Number:
7

Body Part:
lungs

Flowers:
honeysuckle, jasmine

Your Personal Power:
sense of humor

What You Have to Learn:
how to live through your heart

What Men Adore About You:
your scintillating wit

The Positive You

The queen of communication, you are a clever, witty girl who sparkles with personality. Smart, fast, glib, and utterly persuasive, you know a little about a lot of subjects and can pull it all together in a flash. You're simply dazzling and a must at dinner parties, where you carry the conversation among the dullest of people.

Your curiosity steers you in diverse directions. You soak up all sorts of information everywhere you go. Is it any wonder you're so interesting to others? You're so *interested* in so many subjects, people, and places. Life seems like a whirlwind of fascinating discoveries when *you're* around! Restless and ever inquisitive, you are always imagining what *might* be—and always making life into an open-ended adventure.

Variety entices you. Mental challenges make you come alive. And as a result, you are more prone to emotional game-playing than many of your astrological sisters. When boredom strikes, and it can quite easily, you can turn almost anything into a contest. You are at your best when you're being amused or stimulated, and you have a fun-loving personality that can be both entertaining and enlightening. You love to come across a new writer, style, food, philosophy, piece of music—and share it. Your ability to communicate your new ideas and discoveries makes you an excellent teacher and facilitator. In addition, you have a natural writing ability that more often than not begs to be expressed.

Born under the sign of the twins, you have many different sides to your personality—all of which seek expression at one time or another. You are drawn to people who mirror your smarts, changeability, and eagerness to learn. To you, information is power. So naturally, you are quite impressed by people who are well informed, well read and well educated. However, you are purely *galvanized* by anyone who's witty, clever repartee makes you look tongue-tied by comparison. You admire leaders who command respect through their intellect and are most attracted to men who immediately and cleverly impress you. Being impressed is one of your favorite things. It is right up there with having an "exciting new experience" and meeting a "fascinating new person."

Naturally gregarious, you love to go to parties, dinners, museums, and galas. Your vision of the great life is constant action and interaction with a large assortment of interesting people at "happening" events. Without stimulation for your mercurial nature, you can get restless, moody, and distracted.

The changeable quality in your personality also makes you flexible and adaptable. When a problem arises, you can quickly shift gears and try a different approach. You can tolerate lots of different people and behaviors too. You're too open-minded to get caught up in negative judgments.

The Negative You

Occasionally, when compromised by conflicting desires you can be a trifle capricious, Gemini girl. Showing up late or not at all, according to your liking, is behavior that is not going to make you the most popular girl on the block. Your emotional detachment negates the feelings of others, and keeps you from feeling responsible. It's so much easier to push things you don't want to look at out of view and go on with your life without care. Or is it *really*? At a certain point, what you've left behind *does* catch up with you.

Sometimes considered "cold," you can be so out of touch with your feelings that you commit thoughtless acts of unkindness. This "shallow" self can also be consciously cruel. You have a tendency, Gemini girl, to be critical and diminishing based on superficialities. When your thinking process overrides your ability to feel, you're a killer! And what you kill is your connections with other people.

Your secret phobia—fear of intimacy—can have you giving so many mixed signals that your lover feels the need to check himself into a home. Dear girl, you can drive *anyone* crazy with all your to-ing and fro-ing! When you're anxious you find it nearly impossible to make a decision, or you simply shut off and cut out, leaving behind tons of debris to pick up.

Ambivalence concerning commitment is one of your key issues. You also have a tendency to spread yourself so thin that there is only the slightest trace of a person left behind. Finishing what you've started can be a problem too. You will lose interest in something you've begun with great enthusiasm to make room for a new project, which probably isn't destined for future completion either. Simply put, Gemini girl, you're a bit of a dilettante and need to develop some discipline—or you will accomplish little or nothing of significance.

Your biggest sin, dear girl, is playing at life and taking nothing seriously except your ego. Sweetness, you *must* grow up. This might not be something you really *want* to do, but if you resist long enough, life will in its own mysterious way, drag you kicking and screaming into adulthood.

Your Hopes and Wishes

These tend to change more frequently than New England weather. Confusion and temporary standstills are typical for anyone who sees things in so many different ways and is interested in so many things. For many Gemini girls, the solution to confusion is more schooling; for others it's travel or changing jobs. Secretly, dear girl, you believe Prince Charming will materialize at the right moment and whisk you away to his manor house. While you take great pride in your independence, you might give it up, at least for *awhile*, should *he* have a chauffeur, a private plane, and a small country estate to retreat to on weekends.

Your Fears

Your most overwhelming fear is suffocation. Your need for space, dear girl, is acute. Any man who tries to close in too quickly or too soon is arranging his own demise, poor thing. His days are tragically numbered. While he's gazing into your twinkling eyes, taking in your witty comments, and wanting more (the fool!), your mind is a million miles away, thinking about a book you want to read, a blouse you just bought, or how much you'd like to meet the fellow who's standing behind him.

Your Strengths

Your mind is like a marvelous children's book, funny, frivolous, and colorful; something you never want to put down. With your quicksilver tongue and engaging personality, you could charm serpents! You are smart, clever, witty, and very curious. Dear girl, your versatile nature allows you to be many different things, depending on your desires. The world is yours to explore and enjoy to the hilt. As you have fun, you become fun. You know that life is not meant to be taken too seriously. That's something we tend to do when we can't see far enough ahead. But you see the mountains beyond the treetops (or at least trust that they're there) and hope to one day get a chance to climb them.

Perhaps your greatest gift, though, is your stellar sense of humor. At your best, dear girl, you make magic. So never forget to thank the stars for your mirth and the joy in your wonderful laughter.

Your Success Style

With your powerful communication skills, you could be a writer, teacher, or professor. With your logical, analytical mind, you could command a courtroom. And with your strong organizational sense, you could run someone else's business. Smart, adaptable, and inventive, you have natural entrepreneurial abilities. You could invent your own profession or start a fad that makes you rich. With your dual nature, you could even have two careers going simultaneously. While this would make most people completely crazy, it might be just the challenge to keep your interest from fading!

Your Money Style

Impulsive by nature and resenting restraints, you can be something of a spender. All those little luxuries *do* make life fun! However, it is one of the many paradoxes of your nature, Gemini girl, that you also have a sixth sense about handling money. You maneuver it, actually. No one except perhaps another Gemini could really understand exactly what you do or how you do it. But somehow everything adds up correctly, and you get everything you really want, regardless of the cost, and suffer no dire financial crises. Unless there are other indications in your chart, you never allow money to make you crazy. Bravo for you, dear girl! Maybe you should write a book and share your secret!

Your Health Style

What most people don't realize about you, you sly little devil, is that you're a closet obsessive-compulsive, especially where exercise is concerned. Having an all-or-nothing need for control, you can take exercise to the max. It lets you feel that you are in total control of your body and it works according to a little myth in your mind: When you have control, you have power. Although this is not necessarily true, it *is* terribly useful for getting you to the gym at least five times a week. It keeps you on the stair climbing machine until you've climbed higher than the world's highest buildings and makes that flesh as hard as granite. Of course, Gemini girl, you also work your body to escape from your over-worked mind. You have this area of your life conquered.

Your Love Style

Although there is no denying you *want* love, you can spend years running from it in all kinds of ways. Gemini girl, you make love *so* complicated! You think too much, and the more you think, the more problems you create in your own mind—so many of them that at a certain point, it seems like you just *have* to escape from them. Many Gemini girls "settle." They fall in love with married men, men who are too young, who live too far away, or who have so many real (or unreal) life problems that it's anyone's guess as to what could possibly happen down the road. (Disaster is a safe bet. But a Gemini girl chooses not to look at it that way.)

A romantic history fraught with complications—some mysterious, some perfectly logical, some pretty insane—means one thing: fear. Fear of feeling smothered. Therefore, intimacy must come very slowly so the tentacles of that fear can be erased by time. Occasionally, you'll have one of those instantaneous head-on meetings with a soul mate (usually another Gemini), but they are the exception in your life. Acknowledge your fear, dear girl, and let it be OK. Don't project it onto those poor male people (who only pretend to know if they're coming or going). They're undoubtedly attracted to you because you seem so confident (such an actress). Give up the role. Be your real self. Find the courage to be honest. Watch how quickly what seemed complicated becomes simple. And don't be surprised if you fall in love when you're not looking—at yourself!

What Turns You On

A guy who is smart, clever, and extremely witty will grab your attention. In general, you are awed by accomplishments. At the very least, you want someone you can talk to. You need a man who is your intellectual match or someone you can learn from. What happens between both of your brains is going to determine what happens in bed. There's no way around it, Gemini girl, how you feel about a man is what you think of him. And if he wants to stick around for long, he'd better measure up!

You're enthralled by the *idea* of a man. He actually may be a total jerk, but if he is clever enough to sustain his impressive facade, he'll get your interest. And as long as he's got your interest, he's got you! Self-possession also attracts you, and a little inconsistency keeps you on your toes. Challenge gets your blood flowing and makes your heart beat fast enough to force a flush of warmth.

What Turns You Off

You tend to have an all-or-nothing attitude toward love, and in most cases, you are notoriously slow to be pierced by Cupid's arrow. Far more intellectual than emotional, you tend to audition men for the part of lover. Restless and critical, you quickly dispense with those who seem to have a bad sense of timing or no sense of style. Someone so *uncool* quickly becomes invisible. You feel you need go no further. You are also turned stone-cold by men who surrender on sight and camp out on your curb declaring their uncontrollable longing.

While you may be impressed by looks and the trappings of success at first, Mr. Right quickly becomes Mr. Wrong if he shows signs of being egotistical or boring. You can never sustain a feeling of lust for someone who doesn't interest you intellectually.

Your Cosmic Compatibility Guide

Note: This shows you how someone with your sun sign is most likely to get along with someone with his sun sign. Some combinations are instant chemistry; some are more challenging and require work and patience on both your parts.

Keep in mind that this is based only on the sun sign. There are ten planets in all, and in a complete horoscope they are all important influences that affect the life of the relationship.

Aries: He is *so* self-empowered that your mind games can't ruffle his feathers—and that immediately attracts you. He's also sexy, self-confident, assertive, and very masculine. He gets quickly to the point, and leaves no doubt in your mind as to who's in control—whether you like it or not. Of course, you like it. You want more. And you're so grateful you've met someone you want more of.

Taurus: While he may be wonderful in bed, the bull is not up to your complicated maneuvers elsewhere. He is the most uncomplicated man in the zodiac, and he likes himself this way. Perhaps you *could* learn something from how easy he makes things (like how easy things *can* be). But, all in all, even though there may be an erotic attraction, your chemistries are too different for your union to last. You need, dear girl, someone a little more restless. And he needs a girl who is one person, day in and day out. Mr. Taurus hates guessing games, and they are part of your nature.

Gemini: Now here you have met your match. Mr. Quicksilver has the cerebral sort of dazzle that you cherish. And you give him the novelty and challenge that keep him perky. You both are spontaneous, funny, and fun to be with. Not only can you make love all night long but out of bed, there is no end to what you can talk about. You're capable of being best friends, soul mates, *and* passionate lovers. Although you may drive each other crazy during the worst times, yours is the kind of connection that will stand the test of time.

Cancer: You are two travelers in different airports trying to catch the same plane. You live in two different realities with no common ground to meet on. He will find you cold and superficial—and with him, you *are*. He brings it out in you. You will find him subjective, self-centered, and incomprehensible. He is—but he would call it self-protection. You both are ridiculously successful at bringing out the worst in each other, and, if given enough time, could make each other completely miserable.

Leo: You are attracted to his grand style and his larger-than-life luster. He is nonstop fun; never forgets the champagne and roses; takes you to the most elegant places; and makes you feel like the queen you've always wanted to be. In turn, you will amuse him with your wit and clever little comments. You can make him laugh at himself—which is something he truly needs. In fact, you're each at your best with the other—and have a lot of fun together!

Virgo: He is too controlled and compartmentalized to attract your attention. Worse yet, his nitpicky ways will intensely annoy you. Your total lack of interest in all of his cautious little game plans will annoy him. This is a connection of no chemistry, poor communication, and mutual annoyance. In other words, it spells instant history.

Libra: Smart, charming, romantic Mr. Libra is a lover with such grace and style that wooing women could be his profession. He is sensual, and he has a great sense of beauty and a wonderful sense of humor. You will dazzle him. He will impress you. And there is an easy chemistry between you, so much so that it might seem as if you've always known him. Once you've met him, there's a good chance you always will. Few connections will make better marriages.

Scorpio: While he is sexually passionate, he is also manipulative and controlling. Mr. Scorpio operates with hidden agendas that hide his true self—and feelings. Cool and amiable on the surface, underneath he is a hotbed of jealousy, suspicion, and fear. He is fun for a fling, but once his deeper emotions are triggered, so are his demons. Your naturally flirtatious personality would make him tie you to the bed. But after your romping is over, *you'll* want to see the world.

Sagittarius: He's so brilliant, winsome, sexy, and wonderful to talk to. It's love at first sight.

You love each other's minds and share each other's interests. You accompany him on spontaneous little jaunts to the rain forests. He inspires you to write poetry. You make each other laugh and approach life with the same sense of excitement. Two free spirits in search of a great adventure, there is no telling where you'll end up—but you'll most likely end up there together.

Capricorn: This serious, ambitious seven-year planner is not exactly the sort to kick up his heels. He's a workaholic who never feels he has enough money, and sleeps, eats, and dreams business. Although he is an energetic bed partner, out of bed he is on a tight schedule—always. This might be bearable if he weren't so boring. Worse yet, he is looking for a wife—one who will be a good mother to his children and have no other life. I dare say, dear girl, this can't be a fate that appeals to you.

Aquarius: Brainy, yes, but emotionally *unformed*! Mr. Aquarius is so cut off from his instincts that he's like computer software. In bed, you had better bring a good book. He is a great friend. He's *everybody's* friend. But as a lover, he leaves much to be desired. Forget it!

Pisces: Intuitive and seductive, he is also changeable and not terribly reliable. You adore his sensuality and the way he seems to read your mind. However, he is too emotional for your tastes at times. What's more, he has a big romantic delivery, but problems with follow-through. First you'll notice that his memory for details is not as good as yours. Then it will seem as if everything you expect him to do is a detail. On closer inspection, you'll realize that his sensitivity revolves around himself. He lives in his own self-absorbed world. This man may be fun for awhile, but he is definitely flaky. So why leave yourself open for a needless disappointment? Let him go.

MOST MARVELOUS
COSMIC MATCHES

Gemini May 22–June 21
Leo July 24–August 23
Sagittarius November 23–December 21

MOST DIFFICULT
COSMIC MATCHES

Cancer June 22–July 23
Scorpio October 24–November 22
Capricorn December 22–January 20

cancer
june 22 – july 23

CANCER FEMALES OF FAME AND FORTUNE

Princess Diana
Meryl Streep
Jerry Hall
Cheryl Ladd
Carly Simon
Linda Ronstadt
Isabelle Adjani

Here is your sun sign's most significant information, which includes everything from your ruling planet (every sign has a planet that rules it), the element of your sun sign—whether it is fire (inspirational), air (cerebral), earth (practi-

cal), or water (emotional)—to what color, jewel, and day of the week are uniquely you. It even includes your personal power, what men adore about you, and what you have to learn!

YOUR SPECIAL SUN SIGN ATTRIBUTES

Symbol:
The crab

Ruling Planet:
The Moon

Essential Element:
water

Primal Passion:
intimacy

Magic Color:
violet

Magic Jewel:
amethyst

Lucky Day:
Monday

Magic Number:
2

Body Part:
breasts

Flower:
lily

Your Personal Power:
caring and compassion

What You Have to Learn:
to be more trusting

What Men Adore About You:
your capacity for closeness

The Positive You

Sensitive, vulnerable, and sentimental, you are a fragile girl with a powerful desire to give and share love. You need a relationship in your life to make you happy. An old-fashioned romantic, you crave the kind of closeness and tenderness that will stand the test of time. Home, family, and children are all terribly important to the Cancer girl, with her strong sense of tradition, love of family heirlooms, and respect for rituals from the past.

The Moon's sweet child, you carry your moods around with you like luggage. One day you're up and terribly cheery. The next, you're down and don't want anyone to get near you. On murky days you create a shell and retreat into it, shutting out the world and praying that no one who looks at you will really see you.

Even on a good day, the Cancer girl is cautious about who she lets in—and no wonder. You can't afford to be open to *insensitive* people. Sometimes your soul is too vulnerable. Cancer girl needs a lot of love.

Compassionate and caring, nurturing and kind, you have the ability to make significant others feel catered to—just by how you love to treat them. You can turn a house into a home, making it the coziest of nests, with nothing but your imagination and sensibility for making magic.

Highly emotional (at times too much so for your own good), you surrender to those you love and see their world through your own soul. Intuitive, sometimes psychic, poetic, and creative, you experience the best part of yourself by connecting deeply with others. You also need to connect with the child within and allow it to play. Let it dance in the sunshine and dream in the moonlight. Then watch what happens to your moods!

Possessing primal female power, you honor the importance of feeling and the wonder of love. You remember friends' birthdays and show up with soup when they're sick. You're also capable of putting your own ego in the background in service of a higher good. As you're a girl who is a goddess in the kitchen as well as the bedroom, the lucky man who earns you will always thank his stars!

The Negative You

With your tendency to be self-centered and very subjective, you sometimes act as if you're the only girl in the world! And when you're down, Cancer girl, your negative feelings can be truly contagious and swamp an intimate setting.

It's hard not to take your moody behavior *personally*.

Because you can be so blind with your feelings and because you don't erect boundaries, you have been known to give yourself away to men who were not your match, who were selfish— selfish scoundrels to be exact. And, of course you get hurt. When you practically shout, Here I am all ready and waiting. Take me! to guys with the consciousness of a pea, they're going to discard you, dear girl. Can't you see that?

Viewing the world through your emotions *only* is like trying to read the fine print of a contract in the pouring rain. (And it *is* the fine print on a fellow that will do you in every time!) So don't be so quick to surrender your soul. Let the future first reveal what it really has in store for you.

When caught up in one of your obsessive-compulsive entanglements, you cling at all cost. You put up with anything he *does*, no matter how horrible, excusing and rationalizing it as if you *deserved* such ridiculous behavior. Moon girl, you *can* be a bit masochistic. You will say a fellow's fingerprints on your throat aren't so bad. At least, he didn't kill you. But, dear girl, do you ever hear or see yourself? You are encouraging the worst in people who are bad enough to begin with! Don't do it!

The bottom line, Cancer girl? Stop running to things and people on the outside because of pain and fear on the inside. Work on yourself! A healthy relationship is about give-and-take sharing, not taking what you can get, feeling grateful, and holding on hoping for more. Grow up and get this point before you do a *big* disservice to yourself and your life, which is worth so much more than you're giving it!

Your Hopes and Wishes

You want love, romance, marriage, deep emotional and sexual intimacy, and the assurance that you will always have it. You also want happiness, fidelity, children, and close family ties. What could be better than celebrating every birthday for the rest of your life with a loving, romantic man who cherishes the ground beneath your feet? How about old-fashioned Christmases in your eighteenth-century country house, surrounded by a loving husband, beautiful children, wonderful parents, stupendous brothers and sisters, and, of course, the dog and two cats?

Your Fears

You fear the reverse of your wishes—that you will never find your storybook love, never have children, and grow old alone. You also fear that your husband will be unfaithful, that he'll fall out of love, and leave you in your middle age for someone twenty-two and ravishingly beautiful. On an otherwise jolly day, a sense of doom descends upon you and you fear that a major life crisis will strike and you'll never recover from it.

Then you really sink into a murky mood and get blue.

Your Strengths

You are loving, kind, creative, compassionate, sensitive, and very, very caring. You're a sensual, instinctual cook, a captivating decorator, and a great lover, wife, mother.

You also excel at crafts, are a whiz at handling money, and can organize and pull off a major fund-raising event, raking in a million dollars.

Your Success Style

Highly focused, very organized, and great at details, you are painstaking and meticulous at anything you undertake. When you finally decide what you want to do, you devote your entire self to bringing about a perfect outcome, and feel uncomfortable with a lesser performance. Being an all-or-nothing girl, you have a single-minded approach and let nothing interfere with your goals or schedules.

Because you are so highly organized and hard-working, you make an excellent executive. However, you're also a natural at more "feminine" professional pursuits such as catering, decorating, crafts, and writing children's books. Because the Moon is the planet of change, you might suddenly find that an earlier choice no longer works for you and change direction in midlife, because you want to do something more creative or meaningful.

Your Money Style

When everything else in your life seems unsettled, money is your security blanket. You're excellent at handling it and never turn it into something difficult to do.

You can balance your checkbook down to the penny, and you always put something aside for emergencies. Unlike many other girls, you're not the type to go out and splurge on a fur coat or luxury item. Your style is to have a solid savings account plus stocks and bonds. And when you dip into your funds, it's probably to buy a house or a condo that will be your fortress in the world.

Your Health Style

Because you are supersensitive and tend to hold your feelings inside, you may suffer from psychosomatic ailments or digestive problems. Ulcers, psoriasis, skin rashes, and stomachaches are typical for your sign, and signal the need to deal with your feelings in a different way. Anxiety is also a fairly common Cancerian complaint—which can lead to eating disorders such as anorexia and bulimia.

Whatever program you decide on at the gym should be augmented with psychotherapy, meditation, and maybe group therapy. Your emotions can do you in, Cancer girl, and it is up to you to find and use the healthiest outlet for handling and expressing them.

Your Love Style

Love means everything! Without it you're miserable. You have a hard time finding life's meaning on your own. Love is a kind of nourishment that revitalizes your entire being. Knowing there is someone to come home to gives you the energy to go out in the world and be your best.

Conversely, a difficult love life can make you moody, lackluster, and depressed. The intimate give-and-take of love is your deepest desire. And because it is so important, you always create it. In your mind, love is your dwelling place. To get it and keep it, you're willing to give a lot.

What Turns You On

What gets to you most is emotional intensity. A sensual girl, you also love to be touched, stroked, cuddled, and held. You adore all the classic romantic touches, from roses and candlelight to cozy winter fires. Next to Christmas, your favorite day of the year is Valentine's Day.

What Turns You Off

You dislike arrogant men, pretentious ones, and those who happen to have bad manners. High-powered men who are cold, preoccupied with their careers to the exclusion of everything else, and never call when they say they will do absolutely nothing for you. You *loath* men who are detached, remote, who put you on hold, or toy with your feelings with bland indifference.

Your Cosmic Compatibility Guide

Note: This shows you how someone with your sun sign is most likely to get along with someone with his sun sign. Some combinations are instant chemistry; some are more challenging and require work and patience on both your parts. Keep in mind that this is based only on the sun sign. There are ten planets in all, and in a complete horoscope they are all important influences that affect the life of the relationship.

Aries: His dash, dazzle, and superhuman energy will overtake you. When he picks you up and carries you to bed, you will feel like you're falling in love. But keep in mind, Mr. Aries does that to *everybody*. Out of bed, he'll treat you like a pair of slippers he's sick of wearing. Mr. Aries just wants to have fun! Although he may sense you want some sort of emotional reassurance, he really hasn't the time or the inclination. (He probably has another date he's already late for.)

Taurus: He's warm and cozy, sensual and stable. You'll cuddle in front of the fire and have romantic candlelight dinners. Because he is also financially solvent, he can make you feel both emotionally and materially secure. Lucky girl, you'll be able to live in that big old Victorian house after all, and have lots of children to cater to and adore. This man is definitely the marrying kind.

Gemini: He is cool, detached, moves like quicksilver, and is terribly uncomfortable about commitment. Since he is threatened by the mere thought of being asked to meet emotional demands, your needs, expectations, and not-so-hidden agenda will frighten him. He will say he'll call, and with a friendly smile he'll disappear from your life.

Cancer: You fit like hand and glove, and you wonder where he's been all your life. You understand each other's moods, communicate without speaking, and decide you're getting married on the very first date. On the second you get your marriage license. Then you spend the rest of your life sharing love, raising a close-knit family, and being as happy as any two people can possibly be.

Leo: The lion is great for grand gestures. Highly theatrical, adoring drama, he'll stage a larger-than-life, romantic extravaganza that *you'd* like to see last forever. However, Mr. Leo is a flirt who likes to fool around with a lot of females. He likes challenge and can lose interest if you surrender too soon. He is not the most faithful fellow and is easily bored by too much quiet and closeness. He will do whatever he can to deal with his ennui—and all those dalliances on the side could break your heart.

Virgo: If you don't let his fussiness interfere with your emotional flow, he could be a lifelong mate. Underneath all his little self-protective systems, Mr. Virgo is serious, stable, and sensitive. He will not only blossom into an old-fashioned romantic under the light of all your warmth and caring but he will also provide a shoulder for you to lean on and be a bastion of support who stands by your side no matter what.

Libra: Charming on the surface, he is personable but not emotional. As an air sign, he won't understand your moods and needs—and may even feel suffocated by them. He likes an easygoing flow with everybody at the dinner table smiling and talking about the weather. Mr. Libra is strictly superficial. He is also a flirtatious fool for a pretty face and indulges whenever he deems it necessary. Enough said.

Scorpio: He will possess you—both body and soul. You will allow him to and will completely surrender—but hopefully not too hastily. Although he will be financially prosperous, this man has a basic problem: an obsession with sex. It takes many different forms, some of them secret and fantasy-oriented, others to be acted out with *whomever*. While Mr. Scorpio is the jealous type and expects you to be completely faithful, waiting for him at home like a little dog at the door, he has no problem fooling around himself. If he's found out, he'll lie and try to make you feel guilty for being suspicious. This guy is tricky. He can wreak havoc with your mind and emotions. So be careful, Cancer girl!

Sagittarius: The archer is a friendly, enthusiastic fellow but worlds away from your private emotional domicile. First of all, he is not romantic in the least. Second, he adores his freedom. He does not want to feel too tied down to fly from place to place on a moment's notice. His idea of fun is hiking in the Himalayas without a guide and scaling glaciers so high there's no oxygen to breathe. You would rather be on the ground in the cozy warmth of your home, by the fire—even if you're alone!

Capricorn: Although he is bossy and a bit of a bore, he is someone you can count on. Stable, secure, and marriage-minded, he also would make a wonderful father. You will mother him; he will father you, and together you will have a huge family that he supports in style.

Aquarius: No, no, no! This fellow is on another planet *and* in another time zone, one in which he is only *remotely* involved with people. He is interested in his computer and the latest laser technology. Completely disconnected from his feelings, he will certainly have no patience with yours. The closest he can come to intimacy is on the Internet. BUT, dear girl, that's where he belongs! So don't try to turn him into a cuddly bear! Leave him be.

Pisces: The fish lives in a fantasy world that makes him fascinating, poetic, and someone who will reach straight to your soul. There's a supernatural communication between you that's utterly exciting. He is emotionally brilliant, highly intuitive, and very romantic. However, he also becomes emotionally inaccessible at times and has a strong tendency toward escapism. Nevertheless, this could work—as long as you let him be and don't crowd him, this ethereal man could be yours.

MOST MARVELOUS
COSMIC MATCHES

Taurus April 21–May 21
Cancer June 22–July 23
Pisces February 20–March 20

MOST DIFFICULT
COSMIC MATCHES

Sagittarius November 23–December 21
Aries March 21–April 20
Leo July 24–August 23

leo
july 24 – august 23

LEO FEMALES OF FAME AND FORTUNE

Madonna

Whitney Houston

Stephanie Seymour

Melanie Griffith

Iman

Kathy Lee Gifford

Connie Chung

Rosanna Arquette

Tipper Gore

Lynda Carter

Here is your sun sign's most significant information, which includes everything from your ruling planet (every sign has a planet that rules it), the element of your sun sign—whether it is fire (inspirational), air (cerebral), earth (practical), or water (emotional)—to what color, jewel, and day of the week are uniquely you. It even includes your personal power, what men adore about you, and what you have to learn!

YOUR SPECIAL SUN SIGN ATTRIBUTES

Symbol:
The lion

Ruling Planet:
The Sun

Essential Element:
fire

Primal Passion:
individuality

Magic Color:
gold

Magic Jewel:
peridot

Lucky Day:
Sunday

Magic Number:
19

Body Part:
heart

Flower:
sunflower

Your Personal Power:
the ability to live in your heart

What You Have to Learn:
humility

What Men Adore About You:
your bright light

The Positive You

Sun child, you carry a legacy of light that you have to live up to. You want everything in life to be the biggest and the brightest, including yourself! Nothing less will do in your larger-than-life scheme of things. You were born with a vision of the way life should be, and though it may have changed shape it still sits in your imagination. A beautiful child with eyes of wonder lives within you and inspires your immediate world.

Passionately believing in the best of all possible worlds, your spiritual energy elevates you and everyone you care about. Born under the sign of the true individual, a Leo girl instinctively understands the importance of taking responsibility for herself. You know that people must honor themselves. Independent and strong, you hate to hear stories of women who have allowed themselves to be abused. Having great pride and willfulness, you can get out from under, no matter how badly your heart may be broken.

Like a child with a pink balloon on a sunny summer day, you love life—and it shows. You lead the way with the bright light of your essence, as was cosmically intended. Your great enthusiasm and jubilance are contagious. Just by showing up, you have a superpositive effect on darker souls. Even on your worst days (you do have bad days though no one believes it) you wouldn't trade being who you are for being anyone else. There's meaning in who you are and in all the experiences of your life—both light and dark. You learn and grow from them.

Generous and magnanimous to a fault, you have a heart big enough to embrace the world. Although you love beautiful things, you become far more excited by giving gifts than by getting them. For you, giving is like breathing. And you do it through acts of love, words of support, inspiration, and impromptu gifts of kindness. As intensely as some people want things for themselves, you want the best for everyone you care about. This generosity of spirit connects you to others in deep and meaningful ways.

Glamorous and gracious, with great taste that tends toward the very expensive, you also have a sense of magic that allows you to make do beautifully with less. When you entertain friends, you pull out all the stops and set an elegant table worthy of a magazine cover. Romantic to the core, you love color and staging, exquisite props and breathtaking beauty.

Your winning personality makes you not only a wonderful hostess but also an exceptional guest. The zest and charm that you bring to a party help to make it festive. The queen of the zodiac, you reign over your personal domain with warmth, love, and spirit. No matter how difficult something is, you make it seem possible. With both arms broken, you'd still reach for the stars. Is it any wonder that people pay homage to you?

The Negative You

Your dark side, dear girl, is something no one would believe or want to witness. When you get depressed or angry, you have a face that none of your fans would recognize. Petulant and impatient or withdrawn and disengaged, you are disconnected from the world—and from the parts of yourself that normally inspire others.

There are times when you take yourself a tad *too* seriously. Impatient with silly little frustrations, you act as if they were *your* exclusive problem. You *can* let them get in the way of truly important things and miss those little moments that would be meaningful if you didn't rush past them with blinders on. Without more tolerance for things, other people, and yourself, dear Leo girl, you stand to lose a lot in life that is potentially rich and worthwhile.

Being too idealistic can also bring problems. Wanting everything to be perfect and according to your liking puts you in a very vulnerable place. You feel not only disappointed and frustrated, but personally wounded as well. This also occurs when you see certain people in an overly positive light and they start to show their shortcomings or backstab you. Suddenly, the person who seemed so perfect comes crashing off the pedestal; according to your black-and-white way of thinking, there's nothing to do but bury him.

The lower level of your luminous spirit self is ego. When you come from this place and are consummately self-centered, you can be cold, rude, and closed off. You're treated like a queen when you act like one, not because you demand it. In this ego place you are subjective, judgmental, and have little or no compassion for the shortcomings of others. Everything revolves around your immediate needs with no consideration given to anyone or anything else. At such moments it's best to slow down, step back, and see your behavior clearly before it brings your entire world down.

One final negative is your need for excess. It can seriously undermine you, Leo girl—or it can completely control you. Too much spending, eating, drinking, partying, and playing femme fatale will have a deadening effect on your life. It will also increase your anxiety and restlessness, which fuels *more* spending, eating, drinking, partying, and overall extravagance. Channel your anxious, restless energy into your natural creativity and see all the wondrous things that come from it!

Your Hopes and Wishes

You want it *all*: success, wealth, and love coupled with the freedom to do your own thing would suit you greatly. Being a perfectionist who is never happy with less than optimum performance, you aim for the top—and usually get there.

Along with happiness in love, your greatest wish is to find fulfillment in your artistic pursuits. Because you are so enormously creative and have so many natural avenues for expressing it, the most ideal life is one that allows you to do this in the way you want.

Your Fears

Despite the fact that you are a surefire success, you have a deep-seated fear of failure that can cause you to procrastinate. It can also cause you to do things that are a trifle self-destructive. Because your standards are so high, dear Leo girl, and because you have such a fear and loathing of mediocrity, you tend to have a life-and-death attitude toward your performance. Anything less than perfect makes you feel like you've failed. You are very self-critical and can tie yourself up in knots that take a lot of time and love to undo!

Your Strengths

You are a superachiever with enormous talent and energy. At your best, dear girl, you are a radiant force of heartfelt goodwill. Generous, magnanimous, inspiring, and inspired, you would give away your last dollar to a friend in need. You are loyal, dear Leo girl, and you love to help those you love. Your presence is a plus in any social situation. Gracious, conscientious, and bubbling with childlike enthusiasm, you instinctively know how to make magic. Your enthusiasm and delightful sense of humor give color to everything around you. You were meant to help others find their own radiance!

Your Success Style

Highly ambitious and bubbling with energy, you set high goals, take on almost more than you can handle, but usually get what you want, and then move on to new projects, interests, directions. You feed your creativity and love of learning through writing, reading, courses, workshops, and your own brimming imagination. You're capable of having more than one career and many interests that also make money. Writing, painting, teaching, performing, and working with people are all areas of vital interest to you.

Your Money Style

It *goes* in style. In your mind, money was meant for one thing: spending! And you do an excellent job of it. You are one girl who feels she *needs* every appealing thing she sees. With your expensive tastes, strong aesthetic yearning for expression, and a nagging sense of perfection, you can go through a lot of money in a flash. And, dear girl, you have so much *fun* doing it!

Your Health Style

Vain and beauty conscious, you know you must take care of yourself if you are to look the way you want to look. Besides, you always feel your best when you exercise! The kind of exercise you enjoy *most* is centered around an activity such as hiking through the woods or walking along a beautiful country road in search of wildflowers. You are usually disciplined about what you eat and healthy eating is a way of life. Early on, you made yourself deny that sinful items such as potato chips even exist.

Your Love Style

A passionate romantic, you can be led around the world by your heartstrings. But alas, dear girl, sometimes your choices are *so* wrong that the phrase "love is blind" might have been invented with you in mind. Once you are captured by Cupid's arrow, you are *all* heart, and that smart head of yours goes out the window. It does seem that the Leo girl has more than her share of lessons coming in this area. Your need for "larger than life" is so intense that you can make a frog into a prince. For what's missing, you fill in the details—until the real details pile up and present a very different picture that you can no longer deny! It is wonderful to look for the best in people, dear girl, but you also have to stay *aware*, or you'll have your heart broken!

What Turns You On

Romantic flourishes can make you foolish with love. Champagne and roses and candlelight and poetry go straight to your soul, knocking out your smarts. "Sincere" compliments, tender little words of love, and lots of fancy restaurants put him in your favor to such a degree that he doesn't have to really prove himself any further.

What Turns You Off

Crudeness, rudeness, and egotistical assumptions as to your availability make the lioness a frosty female. Men have to pay *proper* homage to you. It is your divine right! You won't even acknowledge someone who looks grubby, and anyone who is petty and cheap had better disappear from sight! A man fool enough to call you in the middle of the night and ask you to come over had better prepare himself to be put down in the most direct manner.

Your Cosmic Compatibility Guide

Note: This shows you how someone with your sun sign is most likely to get along with someone with his sun sign. Some combinations are instant chemistry; some are more challenging and require work and patience on both your parts. Keep in mind that this is based only on the sun sign. There are ten planets in all, and in a complete horoscope they are all important influences that affect the life of the relationship.

Aries: This is a truly winsome combination that *radiates* sexual energy. The ram will dash into your life with flourish and style. He will play the hero in your romantic drama, and you both will be carried away by the performance. He also gravitates to the great things in life, like champagne, sun-drenched vacations, and romantic restaurants. He will tell you that you look beautiful by candlelight, and you, of course, will become his queen. In bed, he is a passionate, tireless lover—who loves to love! This could be one you've been saving yourself for.

Taurus: The bull is a bit too slow for your restless sense of rhythm. You are looking for fireworks, while he wants day-to-day stability. You can't believe all the boring things he can get caught up in—and how he can drag them out! He clings to the earth while you keep stretching toward the sky. He has too much patience for all the things that make you impatient. Although he does appreciate beauty, he puts too many *practicalities* ahead of experiencing it. Any way you look at it, this combination is apt to be mutually irritating.

Gemini: You are completely taken with his charming, witty, offhand style. He is more fun than ballooning on a sunny summer afternoon. He brings out your sense of humor, and you rise to it. He is interested in a million things, and there is no end to your merry chatter as you share your marvelous imaginations. Just do beware, dear girl, that this man can be a feckless flirt who doesn't always back up his words with the *proper* action.

Cancer: The crab will crowd you to the point of claustrophobia and quickly get on your nerves with all of his supersubjectivity. He wants a kind of closeness that you're not really capable of giving him and will try to hold you hostage in his shell. You crave the excitement of the world and can't bear being a love object to someone who never really wants to go outside.

Leo: While the lion shares your love of living the good life regardless of expense, prolonged close contact with him will drive you crazy. He is bossy and boastful and not at all egalitarian. You can't believe that a man can be so stupid as to try to tell you what to do. Believe it. He's *that* stupid. What is beyond his nose is of no interest to him. What he cares about is getting what he wants—at any cost. The clash of your egos can be heard for miles, and the more he wants you to give in, the more you'll enjoy thwarting him. He is not smart enough to realize that he's more than met his match. So you need to be smart enough to end the contest.

Virgo: To your way of thinking he is egregiously small-minded. He means well but is far more prudent than passionate and gets too absorbed in his systems and routines. You are a free spirit who loves open-ended experiences. Quick and impatient while he is slow and methodical, you make things fun while he makes them more boring. He drowns himself in details, while you're only interested in the big picture. This could work as business partners—but it ends there!

Libra: This is a fellow after your own heart who loves beauty and romance as if he invented them. He will woo you in fine restaurants where he'll keep the champagne flowing. He will notice your new outfit and compliment you on your appearance. Mr. Libra also has charm, wit, smarts, and sensitivity. In bed he is sensual and loving; out of bed he is sleek, cool, and easy to be with. He is a bit of a flirt though, and can fall in love with a pretty face. Even if Mr. Libra is *not* the last word on fidelity, he can be so much fun!

Scorpio: On a superficial level you might like his mind, but with closer contact you'll find him horribly controlling. In bed he has a devouring quality that lacks the sensuality and romance you prefer. While you like things to be open and up-front, he is manipulative and undercover. His sexual double standard and jealous, sneaky ways will wear thin quickly, and one day you will probably find that you've grown cold toward him—despite his legendary reputation for being hot!

Sagittarius: This witty, winsome fellow never fails to make magic. You adore his sense of humor and his wonderful sense of adventure. He is brilliant, enthusiastic, and, like you, a lover of life. He is also the perfect playmate. Whether you're taking off for an impromptu trip, shooting the rapids, or spending the morning in bed, you'll never be bored. He can be a bit capricious, but you'll choose to overlook it for all the great times you'll have in the long run.

Capricorn: This fellow takes himself very seriously—and he'll expect you to as well. He is single-minded, ambitious to the point of being totally driven, and pretty insensitive to anything but his own needs. Worst of all, he will *tell* you instead of *ask* you, never really listen, and treat you like someone who should be grateful for any time he spends with you. You find him frightfully thick and presumptuous; he finds you far more than he can handle. So don't be surprised if you don't even make it through dinner.

Aquarius: Mr. Aquarius lives in his head. Cool and cerebral, he is fun to talk to, but *not all night*! You could be friends with this fellow and never feel tempted to turn it into anything else. You need passion and romance—not someone who just wants to look in your eyes and discuss love in the '90s. Mr. Aquarius has a theory on everything (none of which you find interesting). The sexual chemistry quota here is below zero.

Pisces: He sees straight through to your soul with a perception that is *too* perfect! This ethereal romantic makes you feel like a child at Christmas. Mr. Pisces is sensual and in search of a woman to put on a pedestal. Here, you both hit the jackpot—and head off into a divine world of your own making!

MOST MARVELOUS COSMIC MATCHES

Sagittarius November 23–December 21
Gemini May 22–June 21
Libra September 24–October 23

MOST DIFFICULT COSMIC MATCHES

Virgo August 24–September 23
Capricorn December 22–January 20
Cancer June 22–July 23

virgo
august 24 – september 23

VIRGO FEMALES OF FAME AND FORTUNE

Gloria Estefan

Catherine Oxenberg

Amy Irving

Raquel Welch

Jacqueline Bisset

Shari Belafonte

Sophia Loren

Linda Gray

Kristy McNichol

Here is your sun sign's most significant information, which includes everything from your ruling planet (every sign has a planet that rules it), the element of your sun sign—whether it is fire (inspirational), air (cerebral), earth (practical), or water (emotional)—to what color, jewel, and day of the week are uniquely you. It even includes your personal power, what men adore about you, and what you have to learn!

YOUR SPECIAL SUN SIGN ATTRIBUTES

Symbol:
The virgin

Ruling Planet:
Mercury

Essential Element:
earth

Primal Passion:
making it right

Magic Color:
fawn

Magic Jewel:
jasper

Lucky Day:
Wednesday

Magic Number:
7

Body Part:
stomach

Flower:
buttercup

Your Personal Power:
critical insight

What You Have to Learn:
to see the whole picture

What Men Adore About You:
your quiet devotedness

The Positive You

Smart and reserved with impeccable manners, you make the most of your time. A serious, hardworking darling, a savior during office disasters, you are the boss's best backup. Completely conscientious and painstaking, you put responsibility ahead of personal pleasures, and in any situation, you can be counted on as the girl who comes through!

Dear girl, you leave nothing to chance! Because you plan ahead, you are prepared for the little bumps that bring out the worst in other girls. Few of them are as organized or efficient as you. With a system so clear-cut it's practically color-coded, you can get things done in the most *sensible* fashion, and never overlook a detail in the process. You love to feel that you have accomplished a task in the most thorough manner. When it comes to getting everything right and in its place, you are a perfectionist who can bring order to chaos in record time! Needless to say, everyone depends on you to do things like fix the fax machine or take care of a hopelessly jammed printer. Practical, no-nonsense, and perfectly reliable, you put efficiency experts to shame. You're a natural at finding the best way to complete a project and knowing how much time everything will take. Fastidious and full of ideas on how to improve an already successful enterprise, you do amazing things with a mess and make magic in the midst of disorder. You have a mind that mentally sorts out extraneous stuff, setting it aside to make practical use of it. It's no wonder that you're considered a wonder!

Humble, self-effacing, and the last to boast about all your abilities, you accept the thankless tasks others shy away from. Upstanding, moral, and more interested in completing a project perfectly than you are in praise, you are down-to-earth and goal-oriented rather than caught in a cloud of self-inflation; analytical rather than egotistical; and geared toward seeing things through to the end rather than prone to waste time worrying about the rewards.

Shy, conservative and discriminating, you are a delicate girl who needs safety, security, and lots of love. In turn, you are selflessly loyal, giving, and nurturing. Unlike many other girls, you know *how* to care, and you do it with an ease that is so becoming.

You're a man's best friend, his mother, teacher, and nurse. You're someone he can talk to and count on to pick up the pieces should he do something foolish. At times you do *too much,* dear girl. You tend to take on situations that require oodles of work. But then you *have* to keep busy, don't you?

The Negative You

Sometimes Mercury's girl can't see the forest for the trees—she gets so bogged down with details that they bury her. Too much nonstop nit-picking is a poor use of your energy and focus. The world could pass you by and you would never know it! Being a fanatic about flaws is not good for your health, girl. It gives you acid indigestion—a condition that assails many Mercury types.

A worrier from way back, you are about as spontaneous as a heart surgeon enslaved by his schedule. A creature of habit, your life can get too narrow, dear girl, because you don't let enough *new things* into it. You need to develop a more creative approach that allows you to be open *in the moment*.

Your bureaucratic intellect can wear people *out* as it wears them down. Don't trust *everything* to little rules and preconceived *facts*. Go more with the flow!

You *can* be the kind of "know-it-all" who can't listen to another point of view. Don't be so silly and stuffy! It takes *away* from your smarts.

At times a tad too compulsive, you can develop fixations such as too much chatter, mindless eating, and nervous cleaning. Sometimes being around you can turn anyone into a nervous wreck. Calm down and *see* yourself—and the effect you have on other people. Take your need to always point out a better way of doing things, for example. Let people *make* their mistakes! How else can they learn?

Finally, you tend to let others take advantage of you and then feel so resentful afterward that you want to take their life. Learn how and when to say NO, girl. It *is* your right. It *is* your life. Don't sniffle and complain. Live it. And learn to stretch a little!

Your Hopes and Wishes

On a day-to-day basis, you want everyone to be happy and your world to be peaceful, calm, and under control. In the big picture, you want security—both emotional and material. And marriage, of course. A conventional one that is stable and sound is necessary for your emotional well-being. Because you are a bit insecure and vulnerable by nature, intimacy and lots of love and appreciation help you feel your best.

In the far future, you also want a family. Children are important because they are a special outlet for your love. And because you are such a great animal lover, life would never be complete without a few critters to tend to. Cats and dogs, a bird and a few fish are obvious options. However, far-out Virgo girls have also been known to keep snakes and lizards just so they could feel a little dangerous!

Your Fears

You fear everything from catching a cold to never hearing from a guy who said he would call. Negative thinking can be a bit of a blight, dear girl, and it will never get you where you *want* to go.

Deeply insecure, you fear rejection, failure, and chaos. You also fear you won't get that promotion, that you might be harboring a dread disease, and that your lover likes someone else. Never fully trusting the soundness of the ground beneath your feet or that your own impeccable performance is impeccable, you fear what will happen when you are found out!

If you are single you fear that you will never get married, or that if you *do* get married, you could be miserable and that if you get a divorce you will be lonely and miserable for the rest of your life.

Your Strengths

The queen of clear thinking and the princess of perfection, you can make messy, complicated situations simple. You impart order with your eye. Artistic Virgo girls are marvelous at drawing and representational art. Having great taste, they also know all the *right* things to do with clothes. Impeccably groomed, they make memorable impressions of poise and perfectly put together self-presentations.

Having a naturally caring nature, you are a

loyal, *enduring* friend who is unflappable in a crisis. You are also sensitive, solicitous, giving, and the owner of a very healing heart. Your ability to act through love is a great strength in your personality, Virgo girl. It sets you apart as someone to take seriously!

Your Success Style

A worker bee, you take pains to make everything you do perfect. You are most comfortable working in a structured environment where everything has its place and you can rely on *your* place in it.

A behind-the-scenes sort of person, you are a president's right-hand lady or the producer, rather than the star, of a movie. Virgo girls who are in the limelight are terribly disciplined—both their work and personal habits allow them to function at their best. Your self-generated routines can carry you through to your goal and keep you accomplishing!

Typical Virgo career choices are executive secretary, paralegal, writer, accountant, production supervisor, personal organizer, conference planner, nurse, doctor, veterinarian, or psychotherapist. A terribly hardworking girl, you get where you want to go step by step, in measured ways that make you feel secure under stress. Patient, painstaking, practical, organized, and usually putting in more than your share, you are a welcome addition to any team as well as a great choice as a helping advisor.

Your Money Style

A prudent girl, you know how to put money away for a rainy day. You were born making budgets, and you have your checkbook balanced down to the penny. You are practical about your spending rather than wildly extravagant, and are seldom devastated by emergency expenses.

While money is almost *mystical* for some girls, for you it is a simple thing to take care of. You make the most of your wardrobe and in general, make due with the finances you have. To obtain those occasional luxuries, you are willing to sacrifice other simple pleasures. For instance, if you really want a new car or a trip to Europe, you know you'll have to scrimp on dining out—and you do it!

Your Health Style

Super health conscious, you have a preventative style, eat properly, take vitamins, and avoid excess. Because Virgo girls *hate* fat with a vengeance, they discipline themselves not to indulge in anything terribly caloric and also treat exercise like a religion. They tend to avoid alcohol altogether and frown on smoking since it is *so* self-destructive.

Being almost obsessed with your body, you worry about your health a great deal and have a deep-seated fear of contracting horrible diseases. As a control measure for your own peace of mind, you'll investigate anything from macrobiotics to making your own herbal cures. The Virgo girl likes to feel she can take care of whatever's bothering her—or anyone else she cares about!

Your Love Style

Shy, conventional, and highly discriminating, you are an old-fashioned romantic who wants to believe in happily ever after. Underneath that cool exterior, you are also a sizzling lover who lets loose in private—with the one she really loves.

You have an all-or-nothing attitude toward love that makes you vulnerable to its ups and downs. However, once you have set your sights on someone, there is no turning you around. You will stick with the man of your heart until hell freezes over—or until he leaves you. If you leave, it won't be capriciously. A life-or-death circumstance will have driven you to it. Loyal, dutiful, and determined to better a bad situation, you are a girl who should get a medal along with your marriage proposal!

What Turns You On

Someone smart, stable, and in control of his life is someone you can respect. The more grounded and financially secure he is, the better.

You are a very pragmatic girl when it comes to major life decisions. Therefore, before you will even get involved, you have to know where you might be going and if it will meet some necessary criteria. Flowers and flattery are wonderful for romantic color. However, you are one girl who requires less of the glamorous flourishes and more of the nitty-gritty nuts and bolts that will make a commitment both lasting and *livable!*

What Turns You Off

Evidence of a drinking or drug problem stops you dead in your tracks. You also hate men who have to smoke. Other than that, unstable, unreliable behavior that puts you out of control and leaves you leaning on friends for advice is something you shy away from. And, of course, anyone unkempt or unclean does not get to step past your front door. You cannot tolerate bad grooming, bad manners, or men who don't know the difference.

Your Cosmic Compatibility Guide

Note: This shows you how someone with your sun sign is most likely to get along with someone with his sun sign. Some combinations are instant chemistry; some are more challenging and require work and patience on both your parts. Keep in mind that this is based only on the sun sign. There are ten planets in all, and in a complete horoscope they are all important influences that affect the life of the relationship.

Aries: *Yes*, he gets your attention, but how long can he keep it? This wild man is too dangerous to be a contender for your serious affections. *He's* not serious enough, doesn't *get* affection, and is only interested in sex. He also has his own time-table. When he calls you at 4 A.M. to inquire if you'd like some company, you're not exactly thrilled (especially when you have to get up at 6). He needs immediate gratification, while you are willing to wait for something meaningful and lasting. But the only thing really lasting about Mr. Aries is his sense of urgency. Keep that in mind!

Taurus: Now here is a nice, stable fellow with a sense of purpose. He is warm, affectionate, snuggly, and financially secure. He does what he says he will do, shows up on time, and if you're really nice to him, might even take out the garbage. You'll have romantic evenings in front of the fire, excited suppers planning your beautiful new house, and a lifetime together with a wonderful family. Is this not your dream? Go for it!

Gemini: This quicksilver sort is big on charm but shallow on the emotional end. Clever, yes, but his talk is cheap. He may *never* follow through! You'll try to make him feel responsible. He'll try to make you feel guilty for not being footloose and fancy-free. You'll end up with a telephone relationship because he doesn't have time to actually see you. Then you'll find out he's dating five other women, all living within five short miles of you—and each other! How convenient for him. What a drag for you. So don't be dazzled by the surface sweetness of this fellow!

Cancer: You are so solicitous when he is in one of his moods that it startles him right *out* of them! The combination of your cool, in-control, no-nonsense demeanor and outright compassion will go straight to his soul—and maybe get him to grow up (or at least act the part). Regardless, he'll fall madly in love—for all the right reasons! He thinks you're the nicest person he has ever met and he can't believe he's so lucky. *You* think that underneath that ever-changing exterior is a person you will *never* understand. He *is* smart, though, and financially secure, and he loves you. So what if you have to baby him occasionally. What's another person in your life to care for when you love caring?

Leo: You and the lion do not see eye-to-eye no matter how you try. He is so *foolishly* self-involved that you think he must be joking or playing a part. You *said* his Mazzerati was *nice*, but he expects you to swoon over it. When you don't, he is cranky all evening and goes home early with a headache (even though you invited him in for some rose hip tea, which always does the trick for *you*). When he starts tapping his foot underneath the dinner table, you actually ask him if *you* are making him feel impatient. But he says no, it is just the weather. This fellow is like a one-man band.

Virgo: You love the way he finishes your sentences and leaves the bathroom so orderly after his showers. He loves that he's met the most sensible woman in the world, the *only* one he's never had to criticize or nag. In turn, he's the only man you could talk to as if you had known him all your life! Because he's so much like you, you know he's dependable, trustworthy, and terribly lovable. Together you can have a happy marriage that lasts forever—not to mention the cleanest closets in the universe!

Libra: Initially, he seems so nice, so polished, and so well dressed. He has great taste, no doubt about it—and great manners. But if there is some doubt in your mind about *him*, take it seriously. All those luscious compliments paid to you on Tuesday were probably repeated on Thursday to someone he met in your office. The scoundrel! This Venusian man can't help himself. He's such a sucker for a pretty face that he behaves like a hungry kid in a candy store. It *all* looks so inviting, and he's so indulgent! With this fellow enjoy the flowers but don't expect him to be on *your* wavelength! He's already on the phone to somebody else!

Scorpio: He is so bright and so easy to talk to that your instant attraction is comparable to lighting a match already doused in kerosene. In bed he brings out the animal in you, for sure. You give him a sense of safety, and even though he doesn't completely understand why, it feels so great he doesn't have to play games he usually plays. Your integrity inspires him to be emotionally spic and span! With you he is tender, thoughtful, caring, and kind. He sees your soul and that is a great reward for the two of you. Between you, there is love, trust, and in-depth communication. Yours is a love that is emotionally and physically satisfying—and that can grow.

Sagittarius: You enjoy this ebullient fellow, but you don't have much in common. Over dinner, you are entertained by his tales of traveling through dangerous terrains and scaling glaciers, but when he makes promises he doesn't keep (as he's prone to), you close your heart. He is so flighty that you can't really connect with or trust him. He is a little boy on a never-ending backpacking trip, and you need a man who wants to be there for you—and you only!

Capricorn: This is your man! He is serious, diligent, responsible, and owns an entire corporation. He wants to get married, have children, and be a wonderful father to everyone at the dinner table. You will be patient with him and tolerate his workaholic tendencies. He will adore you for being patient, understanding, loving, and great in bed. This is a twosome of a lifetime!

Aquarius: This guy thinks like a character in a science fiction movie. You like that he is brilliant, but you haven't the foggiest idea why he's suddenly jumping up from the table. You even forgot what he just said. All right, you really weren't listening. At a certain point you decided that whatever he was talking about, it really wasn't your job to even try to understand. And after three hours it *did* seem like a job! You need someone far more basic who knows where the ground is—and admits it. The Uranus man might be a nice friend, but forget it for forever!

Pisces: The fish *is* flaky, but for awhile he does have his charm. He doesn't really demand anything of you. Of course, he doesn't really give you anything either. Nevertheless, he is good to talk to and you like to have him around. You try to help him grasp day-to-day details. He doesn't. Instead, he imparts some otherworldly philosophy that *you* don't get. You're not exactly sure *why* you still know each other but he's easy to be with even if your wavelengths are light-years apart.

MOST MARVELOUS
COSMIC MATCHES

Taurus April 21–May 21
Capricorn December 22–January 20
Virgo August 24–September 23

MOST DIFFICULT
COSMIC MATCHES

Sagittarius November 23–December 21
Gemini May 22–June 21
Aries March 21–April 20

libra
september 24 – october 23

LIBRA FEMALES OF FAME AND FORTUNE

Heather Locklear

Susan Sarandon

Sigourney Weaver

Susan Anton

Brigitte Bardot

Suzanne Somers

Catherine Deneuve

Here is your sun sign's most significant information, which includes everything from your ruling planet (every sign has a planet that rules it), the element of your sun sign—whether it is fire (inspirational), air (cerebral), earth (practi-

cal), or water (emotional)—to what color, jewel, and day of the week are uniquely you. It even includes your personal power, what men adore about you, and what you have to learn!

YOUR SPECIAL SUN SIGN ATTRIBUTES

Symbol:
The scales

Ruling Planet:
Venus

Essential Element:
air

Primal Passion:
romance

Magic Color:
indigo

Magic Jewel:
opal

Lucky Day:
Friday

Magic Number:
3

Body Part:
kidneys

Flower:
rose

Your Personal Power:
creating beauty

What You Have to Learn:
independence
What Men Adore About You:
your feminine graciousness

The Positive You

The girl who tries to make everything perfect and everyone happy, you were born with a sense of beauty and harmony—and you display it like a blessing from above. Utterly gracious and so very giving, you're like the spirit of Christmas. You make everything in your home look so inviting that your guests never want to leave. Your sense of color and style is something you tend to take for granted. You can't imagine living without beauty. However, others see all your creative talents as something to be seriously envied. The queen of pleasure and the goddess of great taste, you are a living tribute to your ruler, Venus. And as the girl who knows exactly how to have a great time, you can not only get introverts to come out of their shells but also have them start to see the importance of being social.

You love beautiful people, beautiful clothes, and beautiful environments that uplift your spirits. Polite, refined, and always ready to make a wrong situation seem right, you want your private world to be a rarefied place of sensibility and splendor. Quick to see the sensuous possibility of a situation, and make the most of it (for yourself *and* others), you are a born hostess, intensely social, and a lot of fun to be around. You keep friends forever.

Supersmart and able to come up with the most *appropriate* reply in any ruffling situation, you have the mind of a diplomat and lawyer combined. Great at details (even though they're not your *favorite* thing), you can set up the successful business to support your creative vision. Using your instinctive talent for combining business with pleasure, you can even get rich doing what you love to do—especially if you have a supportive lover.

At your best, you have a cool, rational intellect that sees both sides of a situation and temporarily puts aside personal feelings so they won't interfere. Your ability to be unbiased and objective allows you to settle disputes, soothe ragged feelings, and get total enemies to come away as friends. Sensitive, articulate, and focused on the point even amid chaotic emotional displays, you are an arbiter par excellence who could also make an exceptional judge.

No matter what you do for a living, you love being creative for yourself and probably paint, write, or decorate to perfection. Although you adore going out, you can also throw wonderful, elegant dinners that stay in a guest's mind for days. You are a quietly tasteful femme fatale who always finds time for distinctive touches. Feminine, full of feeling, and drawn to all things wondrous and beautiful, you are a bountiful female,

abundant with gifts that beg to be expressed.
Your special task is to use yourself wisely—with
proper love and respect for all the life that is
uniquely yours.

The Negative You

Indecisive, the Libran girl can sometimes get
herself into some very deep water at the most
dangerous moments, just by standing still. Wa-
vering back and forth about what you should do
can leave you paralyzed and emotionally de-
pleted. At a certain point, dear girl, you have to
become secure enough to take a stand and start
to feel your own power.

Often playing the victim, you allow too many
things and people to bandy you about. You need
to detach from the vulnerable, hungry part of
yourself that wants to feel filled up. Waiting for
answers and love to come from the outside is
crippling, Libra girl. You have to get tough about
taking care of yourself and liking it. Otherwise,
life will brutally pass you by.

A bit self-indulgent, you look for a big, strong
man to lean on and use as a refuge from the pres-
sures of living in the world. This will only make
you weak and needy. At a certain point, Libra
girl, you have to differentiate love from longing,
and sharing from a life-support system. You
must take responsibility for *yourself*, dear girl,
and deal with your dependencies before you can
be *ready* for a relationship. You also are in-

clined to be in love with love and view the man as merely incidental. You can be such a *silly* romantic, too—one who confuses love with the security of having an ongoing date or finding someone who will stick around or being seen with someone who is simply wonderful to look at. Yes, Venus's child can be very superficial— and she suffers for it in all sorts of ways.

Too dreamy for your own good, you can confuse fantasy with reality, creating needless drama. In your desperation to locate Mr. Right, you tend to fabricate him, making up his good qualities and rationalizing away his worst. You leave your brain in the bedroom, and it often takes a horrendous upheaval before you get it back.

Libra girl, you have to start being honest with yourself if you want to avoid the pitfalls that *can* be avoided. At some point you have to recognize that the feeling of having ground beneath your feet must come from *within* you—or you'll go reeling each time it seems to be taken away by something or someone from without!

Your Hopes and Wishes

Ruled by Venus, the goddess of romance, you love love. Naturally, your greatest hope and wish is to fall madly in love. Your second greatest desire is to get married. All career concerns pale in comparison. A Libra thinks being alone is like dying a long, slow death in a sand pit. Of course, that's just a thought, an *idea* that you can choose to cling to—or not. A more mature girl knows that there are all kinds of relationships she can have in all kinds of ways. So being "damned" because you're single is a little *silly*, don't you think?

Your Fears

Born under an insecure sign, you have a lot of fears that can interfere with your life. You are afraid that you will never find romantic happiness. You are afraid of making a decision. And you are afraid that any decision you do make will be the wrong one. An all-or-nothing girl who also tends to be perfectionistic, you fear failure so much that you can be kept from trying to succeed. Don't. And don't let laziness stop you from finding a path through your fears.

Your Strengths

Clever and creative, you have the eye of an artist. Insightful and well-spoken, you have the demeanor of a dignified authority. Social, gracious, and a conjurer of beauty, you evoke elegance and grandeur, great hospitality and all the feminine gifts of the goddess. Within you, intelligence and talents abound. You share them with thought and sensitivity, generosity and love. Showing exquisite taste, you know how to create marvels, how to select and assemble to generate wonderous beauty.

Your Success Style

Although it may take a period of time for you to decide what you really want to do, once committed you work with full abandon. In terms of career choice, you are at home in anything creative, from painting and sculpting to writing or photography. Fashion design and interior decorating are also areas that could bring success. Since Libra is the sign of law, lots of lawyers fall under this sign. Whether you know it or not, you have strong negotiating skills and can bring both sides together to create a win-win outcome.

Your Money Style

Libra girl, you cannot resist all those little luxuries that make life worthwhile! Unfortunately, you pay the price with an unbalanced budget that can begin to overwhelm you. Because you have excellent taste, however, you find it quite difficult to settle for second best or go the more prudent route of simply buying less. A sense of the lavish adds a definite luster to your life that can be addictive. A tendency to spend money for emotional reasons—those murky moods that won't respond to a cup of tea—can get you into trouble too. So once again, be self-aware!

Your Health Style

While the Libra girl loves to look good, she is also a trifle self-indulgent when it comes to the healthy pursuit of pleasure. This includes a penchant for fine wine, an overly developed sweet tooth, and a feeling that she might faint if she forced herself to go to the gym in a foul mood. Libra is a sign known far more for excess than macrobiotic diets. And in terms of exercise, the only consistency seems to be complete inconsistency.

Your Love Style

An old-fashioned romantic, you are in love with love and all the romantic gestures that make you feel as if you're starring in the midnight movie. Love *must* be sublime. You'll even take it short-lived, as long as it is mindbendingly romantic. You love love that is blind and terribly glamorous. But if you can't get the glamour, you make do with drama, passion, or enough pain to at least remember it with longing.

What Turns You On

It is beauty, not character, that initially blindsides you. While for some, beauty is only in the eye of the beholder, for you it is an objective aesthetic, something *out there* that you want to take in. As a result, flashy fellows are the first to get your attention; the more overall pizzazz they have, the better. You are most attracted to men who not only look good but who also act the part; to flourishing romantic gestures such as dinners by candlelight, champagne by the sea, and roses every day of the week. Essentially, you love displays of sensitivity and sensuality, with the underlying guideline being the grander the better.

What Turns You Off

Crudeness, rudeness, and contemptible surroundings stop the message to your brain that this somehow might do. When in love, the Libra woman will put up with a lot of selfish behavior for the sake of saving a situation she needs. However, first impressions *are* persuasive. If a man does not make an attempt to make himself attractive to you initially, he might as well forget going further.

Your Cosmic Compatibility Guide

Note: This shows you how someone with your sun sign is most likely to get along with someone with his sun sign. Some combinations are instant chemistry; some are more challenging and require work and patience on both your parts. Keep in mind that this is based only on the sun sign. There are ten planets in all, and in a complete horoscope they are all important influences that affect the life of the relationship.

Aries: This is infatuation from the start. He fits your image of the big, brave hero. He is passionate, romantic, and very convincing. The problem is that he is also inconsistent, a roué and an ego-tistical bully who has to have his way. Your old pattern, where such larger-than-life energy comes at you, is to allow yourself to be pushed around. Don't. When he behaves badly, stand up to him and say NO! He'll probably stop and maybe even start to respect you.

Taurus: This is a reasonable fellow who likes the good life and all the creature comforts that go with it. You share a sense of beauty that suits you both. You find him to be solid and *dependable*. He finds you physically attractive, witty, and nice. He is sensual, passionate, and loyal. To-gether, you'll enjoy many lazy, happy, quiet times that make you feel nourished and secure. This connection *could* happily last a lifetime!

Gemini: This flirty fellow will be like a merry flight of fancy. He is witty, wonderful, magical, and *sees* so much! He will love your sense of hu-mor; you will love how he inspires it. The two of you will get lost in chatter, laughter, meaning-ful conversation, and lots of lovemaking. You bring beauty into his life. He makes sure your life is never boring. There is only one thing you have to watch: take special care that you don't drown him in your insecurities. This is not a man you can *lean* on. He is all air and easily suffo-cated. When pulled down by too much heavy emotion, he will take flight and do a very clever disappearing act in his mercurial way.

Cancer: You will find his subjectivity something you don't even *want* to try to understand. His moods demand that he be catered to. And even though this is something that is easy for you to do, you get sick of doing it—when nothing is given in exchange. You need someone you can talk to and share with, not a child you have to coddle. His extreme self-centeredness will make you feel lonely even in your most beautiful dress at an elegant candlelight dinner. Keep in mind, Libra girl, that you are only one person and you can't fill in the other half!

Leo: You lose your heart to his grand gestures and fall in love with his larger-than-life style. You both adore romance for the sake of romance and can outdo the other in living life to the fullest. He is the knight in shining armor that you've always dreamed of. You are the beautiful princess he can protect, love, cherish, and for whom he can act out the role of great lover. Together you can create your own glossy world that supports your vision of the way life *should* be!

Virgo: He thinks you're charming and delightful. You think he's boring, stuffy, and constrictive. His idea of a great time is working up a cost analysis for a couch. Your idea of a great time is going to a lavish party with lots of fascinating people. He'll study your champagne glass for water spots and criticize you for all the money you spend. You can't believe how little beauty he sees in life; he can't believe how you see everything so unrealistically. In other words, you two could be the couple from hell.

Libra: You are soul mates on a beautiful desert island. Together you make romance, love, laughter, and have lots of fun-filled moments. You each know what the other is thinking, outdo each other with delicate, thoughtful gestures, and enjoy luscious quiet time all alone. Needless to say, soon after you set eyes on each other, you're inseparable. How wonderful!

Scorpio: Unless he's uniquely *evolved*, this fellow will prove to be tricky business for you. He needs to control, own, and dominate far more than he needs to love. While smiling sweetly, he will manipulate you, pulling strings you didn't even know you had. You excite him with all the beauty you bring with you but *beware*. You don't need his mind games, dear girl, or his double standard, the one that has him possessing you completely while he cavorts with other damsels on the side. You need to be able to *trust*! And he can be underhanded.

Sagittarius: He is terribly jolly and amusing. You adore his wild enthusiasm and dash-about style. However, when he forgets to show up for your date because he has so much going on, you're not charmed. Yes, he can be more fun than ballooning on a beautiful summer day, but he is not reliable. Mr. Sag. is a man of the moment with a very short attention span and terribly selective memory. He, of course, forgets whatever he fears will bind him. And at a certain point, you *will* want to bind him, my dear. If you just keep it to yourself, he might hang around for awhile.

Capricorn: Now here is a reliable, solid fellow who *follows up!* Hardworking, nose to the ground, business *way* before pleasure, he can also be a bit boring. He'll discuss his business deals by candlelight and ask you why you didn't wear your *other* dress. As long as he's in your life he feels he has a right play the *patriarch!* And Mr. Cap. can be *so* insensitive to all those little subtleties that so matter to you. He does appreciate the finer things in life but values *things* over people. If you are beautiful, conciliatory, and smooth his feathers, he may give you a diamond, but at what a *price!*

Aquarius: He is an affable, friendly fellow who is perfectly fine for a few little chats. However, he is so lost in his own head that you practically have to tie him down to get some *physical* attention. His idea of intimacy is to stay up all night discussing technology. But you need passion and romance and *personal* attention, not 3 A.M. lectures on the big bang theory.

Pisces: In bed he knows just what to do with your body. Out of bed, he seems to speak to your soul. In record time you will decide you want to keep him forever. Just keep in mind that there are a lot of women in his past—and probably in his present. Mr. Pisces is unconsciously duplicitous. He doesn't even *realize* that there's anything wrong with two dates in the same evening. After all, he likes you both! This man is made more for *universal* love, and since he changes from day to day, it's hard to know who you're *really* dealing with.

MOST MARVELOUS
COSMIC MATCHES

Leo July 24–August 23
Gemini May 22–June 21
Libra September 24–October 23

MOST DIFFICULT
COSMIC MATCHES

Virgo August 24–September 23
Cancer June 22–July 23
Pisces February 20–March 20

s c o r p i o
october 24 – november 22

SCORPIO FEMALES OF FAME AND FORTUNE

Demi Moore

Julia Roberts

Jodie Foster

Meg Ryan

Winona Ryder

Nicollette Sheridan

Sean Young

Jaclyn Smith

Maria Shriver

Tatum O'Neal

Bo Derek

Linda Evans

Here is your sun sign's most significant information, which includes everything from your ruling planet (every sign has a planet that rules it), the element of your sun sign—whether it is fire (inspirational), air (cerebral), earth (practical), or water (emotional)—to what color, jewel, and day of the week are uniquely you. It even includes your personal power, what men adore about you, and what you have to learn!

YOUR SPECIAL SUN SIGN ATTRIBUTES

Symbols:
The scorpion, the eagle, and the dove

Ruling Planets:
Pluto and Mars

Essential Element:
water

Primal Passions:
power and passion

Magic Colors:
black and purple

Magic Jewel:
onyx

Lucky Day:
Tuesday

Magical Number:
8

Body Parts:
large intestine and reproductive system

Flower:
geranium

Your Personal Power:
depth

What You Have to Learn:
transformation

What Men Adore About You:
your sexual magnetism

The Positive You

A girl of mystery and magnetism, you have an overall allure that no one can forget. Emotionally intense and complex, there is so much beneath the surface with you, and no one ever sees it. You are an intricately interwoven tapestry. People are often perplexed by you—or think they *completely* know you when they really haven't a clue. All they know is what you *allow* them to know. You are anything but an open book!

Bright, shrewd, and deeply intuitive, you can see through people at a glance. And since you're analytical too, anything you don't understand immediately you can figure out later on—should you be so interested. A Scorpio girl is not initially taken with too many people—most seem too shallow and silly for your taste. You prefer a few friends with whom your soul can speak. Otherwise, you keep a friendly distance and are impossible *for the wrong people* to get close to.

You have a level of perception that puts you in a class of your own—and you have a memory to match it! You also know how to use your penetrating gaze to get exactly what you want. And you usually want more than a lot.

Driven, ambitious, and never in one place for long, you are a go-getter with a highly focused style. If you decide there's something you simply *have* to do, your mental energy could set a field on fire, and your determination could bore through lead walls. Girl, you can be one formidable force! Positively energized, you can pull off anything—without really struggling. You simply burn up the opposition with your megawatt mind!

Drawn to people who are as intense and deep as you are, you have a fascination for difficult men who make you stretch or who *you* try to make over. You're a sucker for smoldering eye contact across a crowded room. Caught in the throes of a great passion, you would not be aware of a gun at your ear *and* a knife at your throat. You couldn't care less about death at such a moment. And you seem to require many of those moments.

Having an intensely passionate nature that *needs* release, you are drawn to consuming attractions like a moth to a flame. And when they don't exist, you get very, very bored, have a few glasses of champagne, and create them. Your legendary sexuality is intricately tied to your emotional makeup. The more drama, danger, and challenge, the sexier you are.

You love to be possessed, dear girl. You are either compulsively attracted or cold as ice. Of course, there are some Scorpio girls who grow up and grow out of their need for all the Sturm und Drang and fireworks displays. They have done it all and seen it all and now want something *sweet* like caring and kindness. Yes, it *is* true. And watch out, it might happen to you!

The Negative You

There is a dark side to you, dear girl, and it follows you around like a shadow. Moodiness and emotionally black moments that seem to come from nowhere *can* be immobilizing before they mysteriously float away.

Your obsessive-compulsive personality can steer you in self-destructive directions. You're often attracted to what's wrong for you and can't let go until you've gone through a mini death and rebirth. Only a Scorpio girl can get so *down*, because only a Scorpio girl has such *depth*. That kind of emotional *pain*, dear girl, *can* be a stepping stone to your higher power!

Given to excess and throes of jealousy and suspicion, you can be *wicked* when you act on your lower feelings. Sarcastic, cruel, and capable of undermining anyone who evokes those feelings, you can be ruthless and brilliantly manipulative, very vindictive and willing to hold on to a grudge for years if necessary. With a sense of supreme justice, you will get your revenge. What you fail to realize, Scorpio girl, is that your negativity *owns* you. You are a *victim* of the desire for vengeance and are haunted by it. You need to learn how to *release* yourself from hurtful circumstances so they won't clog your insides. This energy turned in a *positive* direction will work *for* you rather than against you. So isn't it worthwhile to *try* to get out from beneath its grasp?

Your need for power games and power plays is a silly reaction to fear. You get strong from power *within*, not by wielding power *over*. Think to yourself, *In twenty years, who will care how many men I've seduced or enslaved? Who will care about power at the office and what I had to do to get it?* Will it really give your life *meaning*? I hope not, dear girl, for *your* sake. You're a *Scorpio*, so there's so much more to you than *that*! What's more, whatever you choose to ignore *will* get you in the end!

Your Hopes and Wishes

Your first wish is a relationship that will satisfy you both emotionally and sexually. The Scorpio girl is not happiest going it alone. She usually has at least one fellow on a string willing to serve her needs.

Your second wish is for fulfillment in your chosen career. Having her sense of power frustrated is most painful for a Scorpio girl. You need to see your achievements played back to you and affirmed in the outside world.

Your third wish is to get beyond your moods and fears; to live a lighter, less complicated day-to-day life.

Your Fears

Your most deep-seated fear is the fear of abandonment. Ironically, a big abandonment crisis usually does occur at some point in your life.

Next in line is your fear of death—your obsession with it, really. You *are* the deepest, most complicated sign, girl, and so you become preoccupied with some very heavy thoughts!

Finally you fear that some dread disease or disaster will grab you from behind. Scorpio girl, you need to feel in control at all times (except in bed). Your imagination can make demons emerge from dark places. But take it easy, girl, none of them are *real*. No matter what negative turns you take in your mind, you can always learn to undo them! Now isn't that a relief!

Your Strengths

You have enormous determination and a fierce inner sense of purpose along with willpower that makes other girls look frail by comparison.

You are also enormously intelligent, emotionally deep, and very, very perceptive. Your analytical ability could be put to great use on Wall Street or as a psychoanalyst!

Last, but certainly not least, you are a loyal, devoted friend who can be self-sacrificing when the situation demands it. Your ability to love runs *deep*—whether it's for a friend, family member, or lover.

Of course, you're also sexy and *magnetic*, Scorpio girl, but that goes without saying because *everybody* knows *that!*

Your Success Style

You'll make it to the top because you are very smart, organized, disciplined, and because you plan ahead! You are also very shrewd and have a penchant for power plays that can work for or against you. So be careful!

You have focus that could eclipse a brain surgeon's. As a matter of fact, you could *be* a brain surgeon. You could also be a financial analyst, a psychoanalyst, a movie producer, or a successful entrepreneur.

One thing you cannot do for very long is be ordered around by idiots or *anyone* who does not respect your gifts and give you personal encouragement. So hopefully, when you reach the top, Scorpio girl, you will handle your power responsibly.

Your Money Style

You are very shrewd with money and instinctively know how to handle it in a way that empowers you. Scorpio girls who get carried away because they need so many power props usually can always pull themselves back into place—if they *have* to.

Scorpio is the sign of finance and many girls make a bundle. Successful Scorpio girls have all sorts of investments and know that making money *from* their money is often more important than spending it on something momentarily satisfying.

Your Health Style

You are prone to gynecological–type infections and intestinal irritations and tend to internalize intense emotions so that they get released physically. Your number one problem area is anger—and how it affects your body. Deep, complex Scorpio girls benefit from psychotherapy and the sort of physical sublimation that *gets out* negative emotion. Raquetball, tennis, and dancing out your emotions to all different kinds of music, whether alone or with someone else, can make a noticeable difference.

It's also important to be conscious of what you're *really* feeling in various situations. Many Scorpio girls block their emotions in the moment and have delayed reactions to hurt or rage. Later on, when they get depressed or sick, they have no idea why. If you start watching your own reactions now, you can save on medical bills down the road!

Your Love Style

Intensely emotional and sexually passionate, you can get involved in tornado-like affairs that swoop you up and hurl you through space. Born under the sign of sex, you've witnessed its divine mysteries with your own body. However it is red-hot passion, not mere sex, that captivates you. The kind of passion that makes you lose your mind and puts you in a fog all through the workday is your favorite way of having a good time. You want to smolder and then burst into flame like a rocket launching. The only unfortunate thing is that it's rarely the nice guys who have this chemical effect on your libido. There has to be a little danger, a challenge, an on-the-edge quality before your nerve endings start to quiver.

And so, addictive affairs—those that ensnare you and those that you create—are right up your alley. It takes quite a few years before you are ready for "mature" love and see that all those passions usually end up in emptiness. However, whether the love is mature or merely addictive, it is something you *have* to have! You will spend a lifetime probing its mysteries and still find you don't understand it.

What Turns You On

Smoldering glances across a crowded room, mystery, intrigue, the feeling of heat days later. Also sexual tension with a new man you really *want*, fantasies, forgetting that you have to be somewhere because you have lost track of the time, the day, the month, and the year. Suddenly remembering and not caring.

What Turns You Off

Men who are weak or whiny. Men who never get your signals. Men who wouldn't think to give signals. Men who seem married to wives who are their mothers. Men who come to you for comfort, nurturance, and support. Men who are clingy and cloying and get in your way instead of grabbing you!

Your Cosmic Compatibility Guide

Note: This shows you how someone with your sun sign is most likely to get along with someone with his sun sign. Some combinations are instant chemistry; some are more challenging and require work and patience on both your parts. Keep in mind that this is based only on the sun sign. There are ten planets in all, and in a complete horoscope they are all important influences that affect the life of the relationship.

Aries: This is fireworks from the start. You will instantaneously get each other's attention—even if you're both late for work. The sexual collision will take you into outer space. That's great. But what happens when you're back on *earth*? Well, the ram is quite a selfish fellow. Should he decide that you are a marvelous dessert that he'd like to try again, he will be so pulled in and overwhelmed by your real sexual and emotional power that he *may* try to undermine you. The ram is *not* a big boy. And nothing in his life has ever told him that he had to be. He plays nasty games when threatened, and you're just the powerful girl to threaten him. Chances are that he is not your hero.

Taurus: He is a sweet, cuddly fellow and you are terribly fond of him, but you're on completely different wavelengths. He could never give you the kind of razor's edge insanity you crave when you get restless. There is also no basis for communication. The bull goes for what is solid, concrete, and obvious (as in "I see a steak right here before me. Yes!") Your depth has no place here. You would have to go and brood in the basement while he watches TV and never misses a commercial. *Boring!*

Gemini: He is so clever, witty, and verbally facile that you feel instantly interested. He is also good in bed, and that makes him even more to your liking. But after awhile, he *can* wear thin because he is so superficial. He is also emotionally detached, ambivalent about commitment, and a flirty kind of fellow with a bevy of females in tow. Although he could be entertaining for awhile, Mr. Gemini is not the sort of soul mate that you crave.

Cancer: Even though this is *not* mindless passion from the start, it does have *long-term* possibility. The crab is intuitive and smart, affectionate and full of love. He is also loyal. He *can* be accommodating and is definitely caring. Not a bad choice when you get ready for a more mature connection.

Leo: You like his grand style, although you will find him pretentious. His romantic flair will flatter your ego, but his narcissism will put out your fire. He also has such a *thing* about performance in bed that it's as if he's watching *himself* instead of being blown away by you. After awhile, you may find all of his larger-than-life gestures pretty empty, and you'll probably get bored.

Virgo: You like his smarts, and initially there might be a sexual attraction. However, he is so boring overall that you could never bear him on a day-to-day basis. You see things with depth; he zooms in on the petty. You love men who are confident; he is full of fear. You like to move beyond your boundaries; he creates walls for self-protection. If there is even an attraction, it will peter out in time.

Libra: Mr. Soothing and Mellow will smooth your rough edges. He will relax you with his easygoing manner and refined sense of romance. On those moody days when you make everything complicated, you will find him a joy to come home to. During dinners with wine and candlelight, he helps you see the *reason* why your negativity is dicing you into little pieces—and suddenly it all seems so manageable, so simple and easy that you know *you* could never have thought of it. That's why you need him!

Scorpio: This is a connection that could go either way—utter madness or soul mates and best friends. The deciding factor is honesty. If you are both mature enough to not even *think* of playing games or messing around on the side (just a few eensy times because it just *happened*) and if you *like* each other enough to treat each other with respect, care, and kindness, you could have the love of a lifetime. But if one or the other or both of you cannot keep your skirt or cuffs clean then pain and insanity will ensue. You'll be two lit torches and a little kerosene in a closet full of rags. *Phew!*

Sagittarius: You love the adolescent flair the archer has for living life. It's fun to tool around in his Jaguar convertible and to hear all about Eastern religion. But this feckless fellow will get on your nerves in time. He treats you as if you're extraneous compared to all his interests, and he's always busy. You are not a girl to be dallied with. Forget him!

Capricorn: You are impressed with his corporate power and even more with the fact that he worked his way up from the bottom. He will give you tips on the stock market and tell you how to buy the best securities. In bed, he is to-tally *there*. Out of bed, he is also there (when he isn't working his usual eighty-hour week). This man is not the most sensitive or emotionally deep, but he does have potential. You could do a lot worse, girl. Give him a chance.

Aquarius: He's like talking to a billowing cloud. He can't come down to earth, never mind go *deeper*. He is so detached and out of touch that you can't believe he remembers to tie his shoes. You find so many of his theories annoying be-cause they have no practical value. In bed he is lifeless. That's enough reason for you to get rid of him.

Pisces: He is a seductive, highly intuitive fellow. You love to talk to him. He is also sensual and sexy, creative, imaginative, and fun. You fall hard and fast. However, he cannot be totally trusted. He has a very slippery, deceptive quality and has been known to weave several women into his life at a time. He is also changeable and capricious. Words of love he whispered on Sat-urday will have a mysterious way of being for-gotten by Monday. For a girl who needs as much control as you do, you had better take care and keep your eyes open for early signs of "memory loss."

MOST MARVELOUS
COSMIC MATCHES

Libra September 24–October 23
Scorpio October 24–November 22
Cancer June 22–July 23

MOST DIFFICULT
COSMIC MATCHES

Sagittarius November 23–December 21
Gemini May 22–June 21
Taurus April 21–May 21

sagittarius
november 23 – december 21

SAGITTARIUS FEMALES OF FAME AND FORTUNE

Kim Basinger

Tina Turner

Christina Applegate

Robin Givens

Jane Fonda

Donna Mills

Charlene Tilton

Here is your sun sign's most significant information, which includes everything from your ruling planet (every sign has a planet that rules it), the element of your sun sign—whether it is fire (inspirational), air (cerebral), earth (practical), or water (emotional)—to what color, jewel, and day of the week are uniquely you. It even includes your personal power, what men adore about you, and what you have to learn!

YOUR SPECIAL SUN SIGN ATTRIBUTES

Symbol:
The archer

Ruling Planet:
Jupiter

Essential Element:
fire

Primal Passion:
expansion

Magic Color:
pale blue

Magic Jewel:
turquoise

Lucky Day:
Thursday

Magic Number:
9

Body Part:
hips

Flowers:
begonia, carnation

Your Personal Power:
wisdom

What You Have to Learn:
follow-through

What Men Adore About You:
your love and respect for life

The Positive You

The blithest of spirits, you bring on your own "good luck" with a positive, expectant attitude. Fearless and filled with a thirst for adventure, your inquisitive spirit makes life exciting. Always seeking and learning something new, you keep expanding your sphere of knowledge. You grow smarter as you grow older, Sag girl, and you have a lot to show for your time.

Idealistic and enthusiastic, you would like to change the world and make it as perfect as your vision. Generous to a fault and loathing small-mindedness, you resonate to the big picture and have no patience for anyone petty. You love nature, the great outdoors, animals of all kinds, and people who have progressive attitudes. You adore being around people you can learn from, sharing books, ideas, and the latest piece of knowledge you just picked up. Intellectually astute, philosophical, and full of curiosity, you like to go in new directions and test new waters. Interested in things spiritual, you are always exploring new systems and ways of thinking that put you in closer touch with your soul.

A traveler on many levels, you can take off for foreign lands on a whim and on each trip, have the experience of a lifetime. Friendly and open with a stunning sense of humor, you make new friends everywhere you go. You treat the entire world as your home. With your marvelous, intrepid spirit and zest for discovery, you can tirelessly traverse terrifying terrains.

An optimist by nature, you believe that even bad things turn out for the best—and you thus emerge from most encounters winning. You also know how to make the best of a bad situation by looking past the surface tensions to the underlying meaning. Born under the sign of higher learning and wisdom, you are able to gain from *all* experience, Sag girl, and increasingly glow with inner light.

A champion of the underdog and a committed volunteer for worthwhile causes, you want to save the whales, the rain forests, and all the suffering people in the world. Active and inspired, you are a formidable force when you choose to be. Your fiery verve is contagious and your dedication praiseworthy. When fighting for your ideals you are most alive—and you have a gift for motivating others. And the cockeyed optimist in you does all this *cheerfully*.

You love your freedom, value your independent life, and have no intention of losing it to a relationship. This makes you a major challenge to any man. You need someone strong and idealistic to be your partner and close friend. Should this high-caliber fellow not come along for awhile, you won't compromise your time with someone lesser. You are one girl who has no problem being on her own. After all, there is so much of interest and so many fascinating people in the world when you make everything an adventure!

The Negative You

Jupiter's girl can be so expansive that she never settles down and finishes what she starts. Fascinated by the big picture, you can snub all the nitty-gritty details that you think will get in your way. And you can be a trifle flighty and capricious, too. Promptly returning phone calls, remembering to send out birthday cards, and just generally following through is something of a struggle for you (one you often lose). Wanting freedom is fine, dear girl, but freedom cannot exist without responsibility.

Now and then, Jupiter's girl can be insensitive and simply doesn't care how she treats people. Sanctimonious, self-righteous, and often too outspoken, you can wound with your words, and take your opinions too far, sometimes even forcing them down everyone's throat. While you think of yourself as a big "do-gooder," you are known for the kind of candor that can *kill*. You should *always* mentally edit your "honest" opinions before donating them to a group. Jupiter's girl, you need to calm down and realize that truth tends to be relative. Not *everyone* cares what you think!

There also are times, dear girl, when your rose-colored glasses can put you out of touch with reality and you need to be reeled in. You want everything to be fun, easy, and immediate, and your lack of hard-nosed commitment can put you at a disadvantage in the *long run*. You'd do well, dear girl, to perfect both your persistence and your patience. They are the ticket to some important doors you want to open and say you've been through.

Your Hopes and Wishes

You are an idealist who doesn't like to compromise, the kind of girl who wants to have her chocolate mousse cake and eat it too. You always have big plans afoot and something going on that you feel impassioned by. Whether you're working on a huge creative undertaking, a second degree (Sag girls *love* to learn), or an ecological project that takes up most of your personal time, you love to be involved in things that are terribly worthwhile! Even if it's strictly from your armchair, Sag girl, you want to change the world and need to feel you've made a difference! You also have a burning desire for knowledge and want to know the *why* behind so many things that most girls take for granted.

Your Fears

You fear anything that could seriously interfere with your freedom. Jupiter's girl needs space *and* time alone to read, think, and work on personal projects. A fervent animal and nature lover, you also fear what might happen to the earth if everyone doesn't try harder to save it. Yet, on the whole, you tend to throw caution to the winds and are more likely to live fully in the moment than to worry over outcomes that may or may not happen down the road.

Your Strengths

Jupiter's darling was born with a faith that enables her to be a free spirit. Cheerful and optimistic, she trusts the positive hands of fate. She could be an example to those darker souls who don't have the same sanguine outlook.

Sag girl, you're also supersmart and unfazed by the superficial things other girls get snagged on. You *like* yourself, regardless of your imperfections. You have enormous pride in what you are able to accomplish. You see your life as an exciting, adventure-filled journey that will lead you to a profound and meaningful place within yourself. At your best, Sag girl, you are wise, a seeker of spiritual meaning and someone who is always growing.

Your Success Style

A fast learner with lots of interests, you become consumed by any project you accept. As fire signs will, you throw yourself wholeheartedly into the pursuit of your goals—even if you do sometimes burn out along the way and abandon what you began. Your areas of special interest are ecology, writing, teaching on a college level, spiritual studies, and travel. Whatever you choose, you'll start out with enough vigor and enthusiasm to last a lifetime. However, it is not uncommon for Sag girls to have several careers with each suiting them for only a few years.

Your Money Style

Your style is to spend it—often without knowing where it went. Far more impatient than prudent, you hate to wait, Sag girl. You want your gratification immediately—if not sooner. As a result, you tend to buy what appeals to you at any given moment without stopping to think about whether you can really *afford it*. This also applies to the impromptu trips that you just have to take! Not to mention dining at trendy restaurants most nights of the week. Jupiter's child might actually *try* to stick to a budget—for a few days! But chances are that the ledger she wrote it in will get lost in the clutter created by the purchases she makes on her next spending spree.

Your Health Style

Always on the go, you have trouble finding time for checkups (especially dental), even forgetting to schedule them. You can also get sloppy with your eating habits. In a rush to get from one place to another, you either skip meals entirely or gulp down something terribly non-nutritional. Fortunately, you are a girl who loves to exercise—especially out of doors. Walking for miles or jogging down a country lane is preferable to being bored on an indoor treadmill. In addition, spiritually based activities such as yoga and t'ai chi appeal to your deep desire for total self-mastery. Being consistent with an exercise program always seems to be a problem though. You are the type to do something every day for three weeks, only to get bored and drop it. Discipline and tenacity just are not your strong points, dear girl.

Your Love Style

Freedom-loving and momentarily drawn to many different things and people, you are a restless girl who gets cranky when tied down. A lover you have to report to is not for you. Neither is a boring, well-meaning man. If you don't have a partner with whom you can *share* the things you love, you'd rather go your own way until you meet him. Unlike a lot of your astro sisters, you are capable of having flings with a lover of the moment for whom you really have no feelings and whose last name you might not even remember a week or two later! Sometimes you're simply more interested in sexual adventures than in deep, meaningful connections. Besides, there is so much in your life to compete with a guy who simply wants to *be* with you. There are your books, your dreams, your desire to spend the entire day horseback riding by yourself and the joy of your own creativity! However, should you meet your soul mate—someone you so *love* to talk to that it's almost like making love—you will be joyfully open to sharing the very best of yourself!

What Turns You On

Someone who is so much fun to be with that you get carried along in a time warp is your cup of tea. You love men who are brilliant, witty, adventurous, spontaneous, and simply brimming with life. You also like them to be accomplished, questing, expansive, and never staying the same. While looks may get your attention in the first ten minutes, looks alone won't hold your interest for long. What you find attractive is the *total* presentation, looks, brains, and personality.

Essentially, you want a man you can *like*. Respect is one step better. And to be able to completely enjoy his company without the teeniest bit of boredom would be a dream come true!

What Turns You Off

You hate weakness, clinginess and men who are wishy-washy. You also hate cheapness, pettiness, and a conspicuous lack of manners. Men who seem needy send you running in the opposite direction. You also turn completely cold if someone shows the slightest tendency to be possessive. Being an idealistic girl who values honesty, you have no patience with a ruthless rogue for whom lies come as easily as breathing.

Your Cosmic Compatibility Guide

Note: This shows you how someone with your sun sign is most likely to get along with someone with his sun sign. Some combinations are instant chemistry; some are more challenging and require work and patience on both your parts. Keep in mind that this is based only on the sun sign. There are ten planets in all, and in a complete horoscope they are all important influences that affect the life of the relationship.

Aries: You're galvanized by his energy, confidence, and superpositive way of getting what he wants. Mr. Aries is sexy and he knows it. He also wants you to know it, and he's not exactly subtle. With lots of noise and self-promoting fanfare he'll come dashing into your life and get your attention in a *big* way. He is great in bed and something of a spontaneous, adventurous romantic. At times he *can* be insensitive, but then, so can you, Sag girl. So you won't be shy about putting him in his place when he needs some subduing.

Taurus: He is grounded in the earth and you're dying to get off it. He will be deaf to your high-flying ideas, and you will be impatient with his careful, thought-out timing. Yes, there is a sensual connection here, but what is there to do out of bed? You both go in completely different directions. His comfort zone is built on security; yours, on freedom and exploration. He may teach you how to pay your bills on time, but how boring! Sag girl, you need someone who sparks your own sense of daring!

Gemini: The twin's mind will fire up your spirit and your spirit will turn on a light in his mind. He is clever, amusing, and full of fascinating ideas. You love to learn and to have someone interesting to talk to. Better yet, you make the same associations, laugh at the same silly circumstances, and dash about at the same madcap pace. He's turned on by your energy and your sources of knowledge. You love what he does with words and how easily he can make magic from the boring and trivial. Both in and out of bed, you excite each other and make life seem fresh and new.

Cancer: The supersensitive crab is simply not pleasing to your palate. He is so subjective and takes himself so seriously that he will get on your nerves in no time, and you will give him reason to. Your brisk, outspoken ways will turn this man to ice. His emotional demands will suffocate you. He craves a close, small world with himself in the center of it. You want ever-changing open spaces to continually challenge you. He will clutch onto your sleeve until you want to chop off his hand. You will hurt him in ways that he has never before imagined. There's simply no real communication or chemistry here—and no possibility of it.

Leo: With the lion, it could be love at first sight, although this man is so bossy that it might not be lasting. He loves your sense of humor. You love his sense of grandeur. Like you, he thinks big and can't be bothered with petty souls who can't see beyond their noses. Your expansive spirit will inspire his sense of romance. He will make you feel like the queen that you always thought you should be. However, after the first few nights, you may find that he makes a few more selfish assumptions than you can tolerate. If you keep in mind that the key to the lion is through his heart—and, of course, his ego—and communicate *carefully* with both, you just might turn him into a more reasonable man.

Virgo: Your unpredictable, occasionally rambunctious nature will give this poor, thin-skinned man a case of the vapors. He is not up to your challenges and tires quite easily when stressed. He sees things in such small ways that you want to shake him, and has a compulsion for control and order that you delight in destroying. You can't bear his constant criticism. He can't stand the chaotic way you do things. And both of you will annoy each other beyond belief. He could be the best accountant you've ever had, but being his lover could be lethal.

Libra: This mellow fellow will make you feel like a lady—and a very attractive one at that. He is an old-fashioned romantic who loves the finer things life has to offer. You admire his taste and his sensitivity to beauty. He loves your wit and shares your lively sense of humor. He is a clever, fun-filled companion who loves to do things *nicely*. You resonate to his style and thrill to his sensuality. Although he doesn't have a great deal of depth, he is so superficially smart that it really doesn't matter. He also has an easy way about him, and will never close you in. A relationship with him will feel comfortable and natural. You can even learn from his balanced, reasonable approach to pressure.

Scorpio: Although this man may make an instantaneous bedroom companion, on closer scrutiny, he is not all he's cracked up to be. Born under the sign of power, sex, and mystery, Mr. Scorpio is also deeply insecure and devious. Since yours is the sign of freedom and truth (at all costs), you won't exactly appreciate some of his less-than-truthful tactics. Although he may smile and convince you that he can be trusted,

Mr. Scorpio is ruthlessly controlling and shows you only what he wants you to see. What he's apt to be hiding is the females he is flirting with (or worse) behind your back. And what's really scary is that this man feels no guilt whatsoever about his behavior. Caution is required here!

Sagittarius: This is the soul mate sent from heaven. In this man you see yourself, and most of the time, you like what you see. Like you, he can be a trifle irresponsible and horrendously late (although he usually shows up the same day). You speak the same language, have the same sense of timing, and are never concerned when the other takes off for a foreign country. Things are loose *and* lively. The king of spontaneity, he has the same spirit of adventure that you do. He also has the same quest for knowledge. Although you may be annoyed when you see your own faults reflected in him, he is your buddy, best friend, and forever lover. So you're willing to forgive the fact he's not perfect.

Capricorn: He is so blinded by the material world that you want to enroll him in a Buddhist study group. He treasures *things*; you value ideas and people. He doesn't understand people; you can't comprehend how he can be so dense. He cares about appearances. You couldn't care less. This is clearly a case of wildly different values. You definitely don't appreciate that he orders instead of asks and can barely believe that he is seriously trying to tell you what to do. Believe it. It's his comfort zone.

Aquarius: You can talk the same language—but he might introduce you to a few more you never knew existed. His brilliant, zany mind will send yours reeling. In turn, he will be fascinated by all your far-out philosophies—some of which he's probably read up on. He'll also be jolly about chumming along on some of your spontaneous jaunts. And he'll be very interested in reading your poetry and listening to your ideas. With him by your side, your restless mind will never be bored. And with you by his side, he will have the kind of best friend/lover he's always longed for.

Pisces: His brilliant, intuitive sensibility will take your breath away. If he is typical of his sign, he will be poetic and sensitive, creative and mystical. His imagination will be dazzling and colorful and he will love your sense of humor. Sharing your interest in various philosophies, he will also understand you in ways that are unspoken. This is a man who makes your mind come alive—but keep in mind that he is also changeable. Well, since you adore adventure, he just might be worth the challenge.

MOST MARVELOUS
COSMIC MATCHES

Sagittarius November 23–December 21
Leo July 24–August 23
Gemini May 22–June 21

MOST DIFFICULT
COSMIC MATCHES

Cancer June 22–July 23
Capricorn December 22–January 20
Virgo August 24–September 23

capricorn
december 22 – january 20

CAPRICORN FEMALES OF FAME AND FORTUNE

Paula Abdul

Susan Lucci

Kirstie Alley

Pamela Sue Martin

Dolly Parton

Diane Keaton

Faye Dunaway

Victoria Principal

Donna Summer

Here is your sun sign's most significant information, which includes everything from your ruling planet (every sign has a planet that rules it), the element of your sun sign—whether it is fire (inspirational), air (cerebral), earth (practical), or water (emotional)—to what color, jewel, and day of the week are uniquely you. It even includes your personal power, what men adore about you, and what you have to learn!

YOUR SPECIAL SUN SIGN ATTRIBUTES

Symbol:
The goat

Ruling Planet:
Saturn

Essential Element:
earth

Primal Passion:
material power

Magic Color:
fuchsia

Magic Jewel:
emerald

Lucky Day:
Saturday

Magic Number:
4

Body Part:
skin and bones

Flower:
pansy
Your Personal Power:
making things happen
What You Have to Learn:
compassion
What Men Adore About You:
your sexy surrender

The Positive You

Success personified, you are a born business-
woman with a will of steel that can help you
scale glaciers. Highly ambitious and amazingly
efficient, you are a go-getter with towering goals
that you always accomplish. A climber who not
only gets to the top but also owns it, you are so
highly motivated that you make everyone else
look lazy by comparison. Relentlessly driven and
fueled by the force of your character, you never
give up once you set your sights on your target.
Something of a barracuda in the business world,
you wither all opposition with your enormous,
focused energy.

A leader who can also be the most efficient
follower, you work on your goals with patience
and confidence, calmly dealing with deplorable
details that would destroy someone with less determination. Down-to-earth and extremely pragmatic, you put one foot in front of the other in

the most resolute fashion, forcing yourself onward *despite* difficulties. You're a highly organized superachiever who not only gets things done but also makes sure they're done *right*. Continual activity not only makes you come alive, it keeps you going. Like a superexpress train, you cover a lot of territory—and it just keeps coming and coming as you keep going and going. Both disciplined and deserving, you are a model of the success you seek.

Feeling you can never be *too* rich or *too* thin, you apply your strict ways to your personal life and can be a little *too* self-critical. Saturn's girl is a perfectionist who tends to *look* for flaws to forcibly eradicate. A diet and exercise queen, you can't stand signs of fat or aging and you have the potential to take physical self-improvement farther than it should go. You're so *super* serious about everything you do that you'll push yourself to be perfect when your "very good" is better than anyone can get!

As a friend you are kind, faithful, responsible, and someone who sticks around for a lifetime. A serious do-gooder, you are always there in a crisis to put everything back in place.

Often misjudged because of your brisk, efficient facade, you are actually a pussycat who needs to feel loved and needed. Although you have too much pride to show your vulnerability to the world, your feelings lie close to the surface. In truth, you are far more caring than cold, and you can be taken advantage of by people who play upon your kindness.

The Negative You

You're too critical for your own good—or anybody else's, Capricorn girl, and can you grate on the ego. Sometimes too superficial in what you choose to see, you'll make a negative judgment about how someone *looks* instead of understanding what's beneath the surface. You must learn that appearance is often *only* appearance, dear girl. It is not a person's *total* performance or personality.

Narrow-minded and a little stingy with your sympathies, you can be so intolerant, dear girl. You put too much importance on money and power to see the *entire* picture, and you're too shut down *and* in to get things right in the human sphere. You can be as cut-and-dried as a financial statement. *Feelings*, dear girl—remember, people have *feelings!*

Status conscious and a trifle *too* power hungry, you can be all show and no substance. *Too much* emphasis on the *merely* material will make you a cold, hollow shell that can only find pleasure in *things*. You'll even trample on sensitive souls who don't *need* to be so flashy or aggressive. Showing your utter disdain and disapproval, you can be both cruel and heartless, simply through your ability to ignore.

A first-class punisher when you feel the need,

you can be a tempestuous tyrant who acts as if you'd been divinely ordained to drive someone into the ground—until they grovel to your ego. No wonder no one wants to be on your bad side, dear girl. You are so self-righteous when your ego is bruised that you wildly burn everything in your path and call it "justice." Too thin-skinned and defensive, you need to take your self-image less seriously and learn to think in *lighter*, more emotionally expansive ways.

Finally, Saturn's girl, you are so busy thinking ahead and making contingency plans for future pitfalls that you don't see the everyday jewels that are right under your nose and there for the taking.

Your Hopes and Wishes

You want success, power, money, status, and more of the above. You also very much want a close, lasting relationship. Saturn's girl is not happy alone. She has to have a man for both sex and warmth.

A superachieving, self-made lady, you also have an enormous need to rest on the laurels and bask in the glow of your accomplishments. In your old age, you want to be financially secure. In the meantime, you want to be *perfectly* thin every day of your life.

Your Fears

You fear failure, humiliation, being caught in public looking less than perfect, murky moods, getting fat, also growing old alone and poor, the entire aging process, and being out of control in any important situation.

Fear and anxiety fuel your efforts to attain the sort of material power that can protect you from vulnerability. However, you suffer a great deal from a fear that your lover could be unfaithful. And no amount of money can protect you from that or from the pain of other romantic wounds. Because you take your love life very seriously, you seriously fear the loss of love.

Your Strengths

You're a dynamo who can create an empire from one thin dime. You have determination, smarts, savvy, and a work ethic that works for you. You act, you produce, you create prosperity while others are home sleeping. You have discipline, drive, and the ability to use direct, to-the-point communication to get your way.

You are also responsible, loyal, loving, honest, full of faith, a devoted friend, and very generous to lovers, pets, family, friends, and worthwhile employees.

Finally, you are an inspiration to anyone who really wants to do something but isn't sure they have the follow-through or the courage.

Your Success Style

You jump in where demons fear to tread and come out with a multimillion dollar corporation. Your megawatt talent for making money, your instinct for organization, and your patience and perseverance put you ahead of the game especially when the other players are high-flying entrepreneurs who never fully finish what they start. You love to work, produce, be in charge of how a project is put together, and watch your accomplishments accrue.

Whether you are a superstar in the business world or choose a creative path, your success will be due to the fact that you never slough off. You have staying power that frustrations and obstacles can't diminish. And you plan ahead, taking in both the broad picture and the details that will determine the stability of your venture further down the road.

Your Money Style

When it comes to money, you were born shrewd. Hardheaded and realistic, you know how to earn it, how to conserve it, and how to make it multiply. Because you value money, it is never a problem for you like it can be for so many other girls. You are naturally thrifty.

However, that does *not* mean that you don't spend. Capricorn girl, you have *expensive* taste. You don't waste your time or money on trivialities. You buy classic attention-getting designer clothes that are always stylish. You invest in art and antiques that show off your excellent eye. And, of course, you are also savvy at setting up a financial portfolio and finding the *best* broker around!

Your Health Style

You were born with a basic body awareness that demands you care for yourself physically. Being extremely weight conscious, you can go to extremes when it comes to diet and weight-loss regimens. An extra five pounds or what you perceive to be some flab on your thighs has a way of sending an all-out alert through your psyche. You're not above living on lettuce for a week if you think it will do the trick. And you are a *fixture* at the gym, the first one there when the doors open. Supersuccessful Capricorn girls probably have a gym at home—it's worth the money and gives them a marvelous sense of power and control.

To relieve stress and as a healthy hiatus from your superbusy schedule, you'll send yourself to a spa. Self-pampering rejuvenates Saturn's girl. And you *do* know how to be good to yourself. You allow yourself the luxuries that make life worthwhile, including massages and exercise classes that cool you down and get you out of your head.

Your Love Style

Saturn girl, you need a serious relationship that is more than a little steamy. Although you may appear cool on the surface, underneath you are far from it! Earthy and erotic, you are always ready and willing when the *right* opportunity takes you by storm.

However, you also need to feel grounded and connected with a partner you can trust. Not the type to enjoy love on the run for very long, you want a relationship that grows roots and assures you of a closeness you can count on. Being a girl who believes in tradition and continuity, you want a commitment that will result in a lasting marriage. For this you will make a lot of sacrifices (sometimes *too* many). For instance, you will wait forever for a fellow who can't make up his mind or give up his footloose life-style. And for a spoiled, selfish "little boy" you have been known to strain your limits pretty far. There are times, dear girl, when you would do well to rein yourself in rather than pay such a high price to give yourself away. Watch your boundaries and be more aware of your partner's emotional power plays!

What Turns You On

You like powerful, professional men who look the part. You also like them to be handsome, sexy, and aggressive. Social prominence puts them in a specially favorable light. However, you are also captured if they have carved their way to the top so successfully they own it. Basically, you love to be blown away terribly impressed and taken by storm. Therefore, with the right person, you love impromptu scenes of grand passion that make you forget your meeting that morning. Or almost!

What Turns You Off

Men who are overweight, slovenly, or poorly dressed need not apply. Because you care a great deal about what people think and only want to be seen with someone who reflects you in a flattering light, you are also hard on weak men, those poor souls with sensitivity but no aggressive spark, and fellows with embarrassingly meager funds. You will also have no tolerance for someone with an alcohol problem, anyone who chain smokes and, the very worst of all, anyone not gainfully employed. However, someone who attempts to toy with your feelings is in for a frightening show. And if he's not very lucky, he may never see the light of day again!

Your Cosmic Compatibility Guide

Note: This shows you how someone with your sun sign is most likely to get along with someone with his sun sign. Some combinations are instant chemistry; some are more challenging and require work and patience on both your parts. Keep in mind that this is based only on the sun sign. There are ten planets in all, and in a complete horoscope they are all important influences that affect the life of the relationship.

Aries: You are totally *taken in* by his sexual energy and are determined to follow him to foreign places. He is the sexy wild man who makes it happen! And it happens everywhere! This is pure, unadulterated animal lust, and, dear girl, you are ever so thankful! He is a selfish, itsy bitsy boy at heart, but *that* doesn't stop you. You'll do his laundry, let him move in, and give up all your free time—until he becomes totally impossible! Then you will put your foot down, turn cold and look elsewhere.

Taurus: Your ability to initiate will push him out of his rut. His slow, plodding rhythm will encourage you to think things through instead of being too impatient. You both share an earthy sensibility for money *and* sex. And you both seek security and stability as a means of comfort. The bull is someone you can love who won't disappear in the morning. He is sensual, solid, and a man who knows what to do with his money. He is also loving, warm, and someone with whom you can spend a lifetime.

Gemini: He says one thing and does another—which is a *big* no-no in your book. This flighty fellow is more inconsistent than mountain weather. At first he seems clever and winsome enough. But when he doesn't call as he promised, he puts himself on your very bad side. You can be hurt *once*, but you refuse to be trifled with by a grinning ninny. Give him an *initial* chance but a very short rope!

Cancer: At first he may seem sweet and very consistent. But soon enough, his supersensitive moods will drive you crazy. Let's face it, Capricorn girl, patience and compassion are not your strong points. You don't mind playing mommy to his little boy once in awhile. But his sullenness never seems to end! There is always some mysterious reason for his remoteness, and when you confront him, you never get a *logical* response. Clearly this is a connection you *both* have to work on, but how can you really do that with no communication? Don't hold your breath, dear girl!

Leo: Now *here* is a fellow for the queen of the corporation. He knows how to treat you like you have always expected to be treated! In turn, you make him proud with your style, status, and power. He will wear down your reserve with champagne and drown you in a sea of cymbidiums. There will be lavish dinners, theater, a polo match or two. You love how he always looks so chic and how his entrance lights up a room. Together you were meant to impress and put the world in a state of envy.

Virgo: Here there is a mutual understanding that neither of you can express. You both have your feet on the ground and brains working overtime. He admires how you get all your ideas off to a zooming start. You respect his control and competence. He doesn't irritate you with needy emotional demands. You don't terrorize him with your impatience. Emotionally, you both seem to be coming from a similar place. And you share a sexy connection that is more than satisfying!

Libra: You love his cool, smart, quietly efficient way of getting things done. He loves your fast, smart way of successfully moving in new directions. He is your model of diplomacy; you are his model of confident decision making. His poise, grace, good manners, and style will go straight to your heart. Your sexual aggressiveness will go straight to a special little place in his psyche. From the start this could be the kind of attraction that lasts forever.

Scorpio: This fatal sort of attraction will sweep you away in just the way you want to be swept! You will become obsessed with owning him. He will become obsessed with possessing you. You'll never *understand* him. But you don't care as long as you can *marry* him. Only *you* could wear down his emotional resistance and turn this complicated fellow into a fearless, go-getter sort of guy—who says "yes" when you propose.

Sagittarius: Although he does make you laugh like you never remember laughing before, he is too flighty for your tastes. He never follows through on any plan he proposes. You notice and want to make him suffer. But you'll suffer instead. As soon as you try to close in on the archer, you're in for a crash landing. This one-man show doesn't need any woman who looks like she wants *him* to settle down. Set your sights on a more sedentary sort.

Capricorn: You can't stand that he seems to have your faults or that he works longer hours than you do. You want to be with him, but he is always on a plane or tied up in a big dinner meeting. On the other hand, you *like* each other, feel an instant intimacy, and have great chemistry in bed. You are both bound to learn a lot about yourselves if you can just be patient with each other.

Aquarius: You want him to get to the point. He never does. He thinks you're hopelessly literal. You are. Trying to communicate emotionally and sexually is like being caught in a time warp. You might as well be alone. With each other, you are.

Pisces: He will frustrate you to no end with his unreliable style, but what he does in bed will make you swallow your pride. Although it is hard to accept, you soon learn that you can't control him. The fish floats around in a fishbowl of his own, impervious to opinions from faces watching from the outside. The two of you are as different as a tomato and a hot fudge sundae, but something sensual will click just enough to keep you checking in.

Versailles from the outside. The people you are
a little cold of and a l...
bu... nothing sensual will click ... uch to

MOST MARVELOUS
COSMIC MATCHES

Taurus April 21–May 21
Virgo August 24–September 23
Scorpio October 24–November 22

MOST DIFFICULT
COSMIC MATCHES

Gemini May 22–June 21
Sagittarius November 23–December 21
Cancer June 22–July 23

aquarius
january 21 – february 19

AQUARIUS FEMALES OF FAME
AND FORTUNE

Christie Brinkley

Geena Davis

Molly Ringwald

Nastassja Kinski

Farrah Fawcett

Cybill Shepherd

Princess Stephanie

Princess Caroline

Morgan Fairchild

Natalie Cole

Here is your sun sign's most significant information, which includes everything from your ruling planet (every sign has a planet that rules it), the element of your sun sign—whether it is fire (inspirational), air (cerebral), earth (practical), or water (emotional)—to what color, jewel, and day of the week are uniquely you. It even includes your personal power, what men adore about you, and what you have to learn!

YOUR SPECIAL SUN SIGN ATTRIBUTES

Symbol:
The waterbearer

Ruling Planets:
Uranus and Saturn

Essential Element:
air

Primal Passion:
freedom

Magic Color:
all colors of the spectrum

Magic Jewel:
beryl

Lucky Day:
Monday

Magic Number:
22

Body Part:
ankles

Flower:
orchid

Your Personal Power:
to understand

What You Have to Learn:
balance

What Men Adore About You:
your electricity

The Positive You

Often ahead of your time and a little offbeat,
you are a brainy girl who looks at life not as it
is but how it should be. A total original, you do
things *your* way or not at all. Fiercely independent and freedom-loving, you fly high with your
ideas and are careful not to let anyone reel you
in or tie you down.

You have your *own* style, Aquarius girl, and it
thoroughly becomes you. Your ruler, Uranus, is
the planet of uniqueness and innovation, brilliance and being ahead of your time. You love
far-out philosophies, unusual people, and exciting, challenging pastimes. A thinker, you run
every experience through your head and try to
comprehend what each one *means*. Consequently, you are a very understanding girl who
is terrific to talk to.

Born under the sign of friendship and universal love, you try to live out your ideals and be-

have in a way you can look back on with pride. You believe in human rights and personal freedom, social progress and spiritual growth. You like a lot of people in a lot of different ways, but are close to very few, if *any*.

You're the type of girl who talks to little old ladies in the supermarket and chats with strangers in the street if you suddenly get the urge. However, you're *not* the type to have one intimate best friend with whom you share your soul. Emotionally detached and rather distancing, you prefer to move in a crowd of people who reflect your interests. You're always in the process of "finding out." And that can take you in a lot of different directions. High-flying, versatile, and imaginative, you are often alone with your thoughts. What you need most is someone on the same wavelength whom you can *really* talk to.

When it comes to men, you need to have your mind turned on before a fellow can get close to your body. You have to be very lonely to have sex with someone boring. And guess what, you find out what you knew all along. It's not worth it! You can't bear anyone conventional or clingy. Men have to respect your space or you send them packing. And too much of the same old predictable thing is bad for your nerves. You need brilliance and challenge, brain stuff and a sense of the open-ended. Otherwise, you have been known to upend the entire apple cart just for the thrill of doing something naughty.

The unpredictable and incongruous get your

heart beating faster! Therefore, any man seeking only *stability* in his life could never be a serious candidate for your affections. You prefer wildness to coziness and lots of change to anything *terribly* secure. In general, the more unusual incidents there are in your life, the better. You like to feel a little like Alice wandering through Wonderland. Adventures are among your very favorite things.

The Negative You

There's no way around it, Uranus girl. You can be *cold* and capable of cutting off emotionally on a whim. Sometimes more interested in the *idea* of people than in the flesh and blood beings, you can be enormously detached and incapable of hearing with your heart. It often seems as if you view people with only superficial interest and expect them to amuse you as a movie would.

Since your ego is as fragile as a robin's egg, you can be very self-obsessed and high-strung to the detriment of other aspects of your life. You suffer from murky moods and an overall intolerance for frustration. If everything doesn't *flow* you want to walk away from it. Not only isn't responsibility your strong point, Ms. Uranus, to you, it's a dirty word. You *hate* to *have to* do things that don't completely suit you. A bit immature, you want to keep everything too demanding or boring at bay. When emotionally detached, you can be inexplicably cruel—and there's no stopping you, slowing you down, or making you *see*.

A bit hard of hearing when it comes to really listening to people, you fly by, skim the surface, and never seem to land. Lost so far down in yourself that you can barely peep over the edge, you don't connect emotionally in any way that has meaning. Unstable and creating havoc all around you, you blame your woes on anything you can think up rather than face yourself. Unless you can be honest with yourself, dear girl, you will never know *real* freedom.

Not allowing people to get close leaves you with a shallow, colorless existence devoid of deep caring. You grow older but not wiser, and watch rather than participate in the game you're trying to control from a safe distance.

Your Hopes and Wishes

Being a superidealist, you often wish for things that are difficult if not impossible to come by—like living your life your way without any interference. You want to do *what* you want *when* you want, regardless of how this might inconvenience other people. A girl of the moment, you like to be spontaneous and free from all rules and restrictions.

Your greatest wish is to simply "do your thing" whatever that might be—without having to pay a price or make a commitment. Ideally, you would be able to walk away from, or get out of, any situation that was no longer fun.

Your Fears

You can get an acute case of claustrophobia when anyone moves in too close too quickly. Fear of intimacy is a fundamental aspect of yours. If you don't take things slow, they overwhelm you. You also fear having to feel responsible for anyone or anything. The great paradox in your personality is that while you fear intense closeness, you are also afraid of being alone. A nice mix of non-threatening people who come into and go out of your life is your idea of perfection.

Your Strengths

A very friendly person who can chat with just about anyone, you have a convivial personality that puts other people at ease. Although your brilliant, original mind sometimes resembles a light that goes on and off erratically, it does give off electric flashes of incredible insight now and then.

Innovative and ahead of your time, you ride high on your ideals and put them at work to make the world a better place. Curious, kindhearted, and fascinated by the spiritual and psychic realms, you explore things that other people are deaf, dumb, and blind to. Inventive and alive in your ideas, you have it in you to show the world what life *might* be. However, you have to do it *your* way or not at all. You're constantly fighting the status quo that holds back progress and keeps people in their place.

Your Success Style

You're happiest working on your own, pursuing your creative vision. Technology appeals to you (you're a whiz with computers) but usually with a twist—something that is your unique take on an area. Because you have a tendency to be erratic and interested in a lot of different things, you might have several career paths that appeal to you. It is often the Aquarian style to do many things in one lifetime so that no one area ever gets a chance to become boring. Besides, you love change—when *you're* in control of it and you're creating the flow that you want to follow.

In general, money and power are not as important to you as they are to a number of other signs. What is most important is that you can do your own thing and have a great time while you're doing it. For you, it's the quality of experience that counts, not the possessions you accrue.

Your Money Style

Money means freedom and possibility. It provides opportunities for you to explore your potential in any area that interests you—and have fun doing it. Although you are not particularly materialistic or driven to accumulate diamonds, you will spend a fortune on an environment that suits your spirit and gives you a sense of openness, space, and light.

Your spending style is impulsive. You buy what catches your eye and your fancy—and that's usually not material objects. You would rather spend money on a trip to some beautiful or exotic land than buy a fur coat—which would go against your politically correct principles, anyway.

Your Health Style

Nervous and restless, you need plenty of exercise to balance all that mental energy. You have an affinity for health fads and new age medicine. And when caught in the throes of one of your "kicks" you've been known to eat only one crazy item like carrots or liver for ten days in a row—until you turn yellow or orange. Even if you're not sick, you're always investigating acupuncturists, holistic medical practices, or different forms of meditation that allow your overworked brain to relax. And of course, since massages make you feel like you've been reborn, they become a major part of your life.

Your Love Style

While change and variety make you come alive, you *are* capable of being with one person.

However, he must be a best buddy as well as a lover, and someone wonderful to talk to whose mind simply turns you on. Because you require so much emotional space, you're one girl who *could* be happy with a married man or someone who lives in another country.

Scenes of possessiveness and jealousy send you packing. If a man doesn't give you your space, you'll *take it,* and get rid of him! As a matter of fact, you could also be happily married living in separate dwellings or married to someone who travels so much you never see him.

Aside from all that you can also be a wicked flirt. But of course, it's nothing *personal.*

What Turns You On

Brilliance, challenge, change, and a wonderful human being you respect. The man of your dreams—or the one to last a lifetime—has to be very special to keep your attention. Looks are relative—you might find him sexy because of the expression in his eyes! A beautiful body is not that important, especially if there are no brains to go along with it. Mr. Muscle Man At The Gym is not *your* type.

Your favorite sort of man is *fun.* Occasionally, he also keeps you guessing. And, of course, he is full of *wonderful* surprises like spontaneous, last-minute ski trips, tickets to the Royal Ballet, and lots and lots of flowers by wire!

What Turns You Off

Men who are mushy and clingy and don't seem to have a life leave you cold. Once you feel someone is hanging on you instead of standing up straight, you turn so stone cold that frost forms on your clothes. Men who are overly emotional are not your cup of tea, dear girl. And men who are so boring that all they do is *show up* need not bother. You also hate extremes and anger, jealousy, violence, or cruelty of any kind. You are one girl who won't put up with the "nasties." It's *your* life and *your* world and *you* want it to be free of ugliness!

Your Cosmic Compatibility Guide

Note: This shows you how someone with your sun sign is most likely to get along with someone with his sun sign. Some combinations are instant chemistry; some are more challenging and require work and patience on both your parts. Keep in mind that this is based only on the sun sign. There are ten planets in all, and in a complete horoscope they are all important influences that affect the life of the relationship.

Aries: His "one-man show" sort of style will definitely get your attention. You're fascinated by his singleness of purpose, and he's amazed at your breadth of vision. He thinks you're the smartest girl he ever met and definitely the most individual. You think he's not afraid to have fun, to try new things, and test his limits! He likes the way you speak your mind and how you have so many opinions. You like the way he'll listen and sometimes take it a step further. Although this man *can* run roughshod over someone shy and unsure of herself, he respects where you're coming from and will let you know it up front!

Taurus: Unless you can drag him out every night, the stodgy, "stay at home" bull is not the answer to your prayer for fun-filled evenings. Furthermore, when you start expounding on your desire to find God or take up t'ai chi, he won't know what you're talking about or care. He has two feet firmly embedded in the ground. You fly through the sky without a parachute. You have no patience for the boring, material way he looks at every issue in life. And his jealousy and possessiveness will bring out the worst in you. (You won't be a bit shy about showing it either!)

Gemini: Now here is someone you can talk to! You'll trade books, share ideas, laugh your head off, and have a wonderful time. Mr. Quicksilver is as independent as you are and has at least as many projects on his plate. His changeable mind, merry sense of humor, and curious nature make you feel like you've found a home. He is endlessly entertaining, never at a loss for words, and terribly lighthearted during those times when you get stuck. You can learn from his mutable, fluid nature. He can be inspired by your fascinating, far-out interests. When you're together time disappears. You lose yourself in his twinkling eyes and dazzling smile. What could be better for this lady?

Cancer: The crab's murky, mushy ways will make you *so* cranky that you'll want to stomp on him and ignore the squish. When you see what this man is all about, you will think and maybe even say out loud, "He has *got* to be kidding!" His subjective moods will get on your nerves, but his jealous, possessive, suspicious *little* ways will take *all* the air out of your sails and leave you snarling. It is far better to go it alone than to be caught in this man's creepy grasp!

Leo: This fellow can be oodles of fun, but he is also rather bossy and full of foolish assumptions—"I like you a lot so that means you're *mine!*" for example. He will dazzle you with a million romantic trappings. But you will quickly see that there are no free French four-course dinners. His intention is to own you. Your detachment will definitely deflate his ego (he so wants to be seen as a big, showy, magnanimous man but is really a little baby at heart). And when he is bruised or things get tough, he can be a bit of a bully. This connection only has potential if you make him understand that he's not running the show. It's not *about a show;* it's about *two people!*

Virgo: There could not be a fellow with whom you are more at odds. He thinks you are crazy.

You *know* he's asleep. You think he lives his life with too many limitations. He hears some of your ideas, and thinks you should live yours in an institution. You tell him to get with it. He tells you to get real. And you both rush to escape this unfortunate encounter.

Libra: Here's a very smart, mellow fellow with a mind that makes you want more. He's like a sexy secretary of state, and very challenging. He is cool and poised, has all the answers, and can see both sides of every situation. Not only does he smooth your ruffled feathers in a flash, but he also gives you lots of breathing room and completely respects your space. And to top it all off, he is witty, engaging, social, and a sensitive romantic who can make little moments breathtakingly beautiful. He could be the love of a lifetime. He could also be a best friend.

Scorpio: You will bristle at his controls and become enraged by his manipulations. His water puts out the fire in your air. Here, the grande dame of truth is up against the master of deceit. And it will not take long before this spider starts his spinning. He expects you to be blown away by the way he jumps your bones in bed, but it feels so *devouring* that you would rather be alone and read. All of his pent-up passion makes you a little uncomfortable, and you find his underlying emotional intensity draining. While lots of women think this fellow is sexy, he makes your blood run colder. The chemistry here is antagonistic.

Sagittarius: Here is a fellow who might know *more* than you do. And he has at least as many interests. You have never seen someone who is so wildly enthusiastic about *so many* things. You feel you have to stretch to keep up with him, and that sets off the first blush of infatuation. His excitement over doing all the things he loves to do is contagious. You are fascinated by his travels. He is enthralled by your interests. This is a fellow free spirit who's interested in owning *himself*, not you. He'll respect your individuality, while you'll delight in his expansive mind. This is a man you may want to marry!

Capricorn: He can be helpful when it comes to putting together a stock portfolio, but in any area beyond business, he is too bossy and materialistic. You feel confined by all the foolish things he finds important, like status and power and corporate takeovers. These are the last subjects you want to think about. They're so *uncreative*. He doesn't listen when you discuss your dreams and the insights in your journal. You don't *want* to listen when he talks about money. Eventually, the little and big insults you hurl at each other make communication impossible.

Aquarius: You can be best friends, soul mates, and happily-ever-after lovers because you have the same rhythms, ideals, and dreams. You can *share* the same space and interests and give each other support on bad days when no one else in the world understands. This is true love, a love that will last forever.

Pisces: His pure psychic ability will galvanize you, and his sense of humor will light up your mind. He is so creative, magical, mystical, and full of wonder that you're never bored. You will share poetry, dreams, spiritual ideas, and wonderful moments. He is romantic and full of surprises, an ever new and fascinating experience unfolding. For the first time in your life, you might realize that *you* can be possessive! Once you enter his world, you'll want to stay there!

MOST MARVELOUS
COSMIC MATCHES

Aquarius January 21–February 19
Sagittarius November 23–December 21
Libra September 24–October 23

MOST DIFFICULT
COSMIC MATCHES

Virgo August 24–September 23
Cancer June 22–July 23
Capricorn December 22–January 20

pisces
february 20–march 20

Cindy Crawford

Sharon Stone

Vanessa Williams

Ivana Trump

Liza Minnelli

Deborah Raffin

Elizabeth Taylor

Here is your sun sign's most significant information, which includes everything from your ruling planet (every sign has a planet that rules it), the element of your sun sign—whether it is fire (inspirational), air (cerebral), earth (practi-

cal), or water (emotional)—to what color, jewel, and day of the week are uniquely you. It even includes your personal power, what men adore about you, and what you have to learn!

YOUR SPECIAL SUN SIGN ATTRIBUTES

Symbol:
The fish

Ruling Planets:
Neptune and Jupiter

Essential Element:
water

Primal Passion:
bliss

Magic Color:
heliotrope

Magic Jewel:
ruby

Lucky Day:
Thursday

Magic Number:
11

Body Part:
feet

Flower:
water lily

Your Personal Power:
making magic

What You Have to Learn:
realism

What Men Adore About You:
your soul

The Positive You

Neptune's sweet darling is a dreamer and a spinner of tales she often makes come true. Divinely intuitive, she is usually so *right* to follow her inner voice to places where things *magically* happen!

It seems that the gods are often with you, Pisces girl, leading you to new realms where hardcore reality plays a very small part. Your magical land is in the imagination, and your power stems from all the wondrous things you can create with it. There is no end to your marvelous vision! It is your magic carpet, transforming the boring and mundane into whatever you decide it should be!

A girl with many stunning gifts, you *have* to use them to the very *fullest* in this lifetime—or you will never feel properly fulfilled! Highly creative, psychic, and something of a natural mystic, you make things come alive simply by how you see them. Highly poetic, with a great sense of color, you inject possibility into everything you look upon. Is it any wonder, dear girl, that you're so successful in the artistic realm?

Highly impressionistic, you take in things that

others don't even see! Your eyes are always wide with life, your senses always perceiving every nuance in the world around you. A supersonic thinker, you also believe in Possibility—which puts you ahead of the game. From your perspective, *everything* has meaning, and within that meaning your dreams are a part of everyday reality. When you want something significant to happen, Pisces girl, you do more than hope, you think it into being! In your mind, you live out your fantasy and then you see it start to take shape around you.

Sensitive, empathetic, and prone to take on other people's pain, you are an angel in need and a soul mate in the best of times. You feel so much in so many situations that it *can* become overwhelming. Your supersensitivity sets you apart from so many other girls who are cut off from the power of their psyches!

Soulful, sweet, sentimental, and terribly, terribly caring, you are a visionary with a kind heart. Your sensibility is like a dazzling light in a very dark forest. Your creative flair inspires, your sense of magic *transports!* Like a top, spinning around your own inner light, you let lesser souls know that there is so much more to life than merely making a living. There's as much as they can envision and create. The everyday world *can* be their magical kingdom where possibility comes alive for the asking. But first you have to be able to dream it to make it so!

The Negative You

Prone to procrastination and easily becoming unfocused, you sometimes have a hard time getting things done, Pisces girl. Being completely mesmerized by the moment can make you late for work or behind in your bills. You have to try to balance the boring tasks that *have* to get done with all the fascinating ones you *want* to do!

A trifle self-indulgent when it comes to your whimsies, you can easily get sidetracked in the middle of your greatest creative endeavor yet and add *another* unfinished project to the pile, putting you in the category of creative cavorter and dilettante. Being a dabbler who loses the light of her path rather than a committed girl who sticks with a game plan, you, Neptune's girl, would do well to develop some discipline.

A tad flighty and flaky and *very* impressionable, you can easily make the wrong choices about people—as well as about how you treat them. For instance, you tend to be overly impressed with power, glamour, and flashy appearances. As a result, you may collect people for the prestige their presence imparts. Yes, Pisces girl, *Ms.* Sensitive, you *can* be a stone cold social climber.

Sometimes moods and mind states simply swamp you, and you give in to them to the exclusion of everything else that should or would or could be happening. The next thing you know, you are in the embrace of someone or something bad for both you *and* your creative potential. A poor judge of men, you sometimes confuse intuitive feelings with wishful thinking.

You also judge cruelly on superficials such as the kind of car he drives or the rung he occupies on a corporate ladder. Your need for fantasy and glamour can get in the way of *real* feelings if you don't watch out, Pisces girl. You need to keep a clear open mind to the idea that your first impression could have been wrong! The bubbles you create *can* imprison you if you're not careful. So go slow, reevaluate, and don't think you're infallible. Otherwise, you *could* squander your precious life on the colorful lies that you tell yourself! There are certainly more constructive uses for your creativity. Don't allow your over-worked imagination to keep you a little girl or make you a victim of your own fantasy land— and the illusions that bloom there like poisonous flowers!

Your Hopes and Wishes

Your most fundamental wish is to get every-thing you want—every single day. Of course, like your sign's symbol—two fish moving in dif-ferent directions—you are seldom consistent about what you want. In general, you want grand romance with a mythic figure; to succeed in a creative endeavor *on your own terms*; and to have a fairytale kind of life in which you *can* have your cake and eat it too! Since the sign Pis-ces is about wishing and wanting and dreaming and fantasizing, you have this down to such perfection that it gives your fluidity definition!

Your Fears

You fear not getting what you want, having to live in the real world, and what might happen if everything falls to pieces. Because your imagination is so strong, you can envision the *worst* happening as well as the best. Your *worst* fear is a fear of being totally defenseless in a merciless world. Underneath your surface charm, you are somewhat thin-skinned and vulnerable and usually rely on strong family ties or a life partner to shield you from the harsher of life's possibilities. Not a sign who, as a rule, goes it alone, you need some emotional padding for the bumps.

Your Strengths

Intuitively brilliant and brilliantly creative, your mind is a source of wonder. You are probably able to write, paint, do psychic readings, and interior decorating. You could also be a wonderful photographer or do a little music composing now and then.

You're loving, compassionate, sensitive, kind, a wonderful friend, and a budding mystic. Talking to you makes the heavens open up. Everything becomes a truth with infinite *meaning*.

Your Success Style

You approach tasks based on your feelings, and your feelings tend to fluctuate. When consumed by a vision or ambition, you abandon yourself to it and leave the rest of the world behind. Possessed by what you *want* to do, you think of nothing else—and your mania can drive everyone around you a little nuts.

Classic Piscean career paths include the arts, the entertainment business, and the psychic/spiritual realm. Writing, painting, music, acting, and healing/counseling are your special talent areas. However, you bring your uncanny intuition to *whatever* you choose to do, and have a wonderful sense of timing—as long as you force yourself to act on it.

Your Money Style

It's a flash of green between your fingers, a plastic card, a signature on a line. You don't really comprehend money. However, you do know what it does, and you like that! You adore buying five pairs of your favorite shoes (a girl must prepare herself for rainy days). And if you have a favorite cashmere sweater, you must have it in every color. You also need at least ten black blazers. Trips to places with sun and sea are a must, as well. And since none of these purchases would be possible without it, you do *get* money, in a sense. *Your* sense is that money is not important. What's important is all the things you can do *with it!*

Your Health Style

A girl prone to escape and excess, you can overdo it with the wine, and you have a hard time stopping anything that's fun when you start.

Not a health fanatic, you do do what feels good when you need to feel better. For instance, stress calls for a luxury spa. Insomnia calls for a great massage. Doubt and anxiety, a little reflexology (Pisces rules the feet). If you gain weight, you're the sort who will jog every day for two and one-third weeks (then reward yourself with a pint of your favorite Häagen-Dazs). Let's face it, girl, you are who you are, and you weren't made to be one of those depressing anti-pleasure types. So live life and just do your best to stay balanced!

Your Love Style

Superidealistic and fantasy-oriented, in a lifetime you will fall in love with all sorts of people for all sorts of reasons. An ethereal romantic, you love to be in love, no matter how long it lasts. (Once you start to see the *real* person rather than the larger-than-life myth you've created, you usually turn cold.)

You are also prone to very painful disappointments. You desperately want to live out the "pie in the sky" version of life and love that exists in your head. However, there are so many things to interfere with that—like stark reality. The prince is not even a frog. He's a snake, and you've been bitten. Oh, well. As soon as the pain of disillusionment begins to wear off, you ask, Who's next? Maybe this time you'll try for a frog and take it in reverse, believing that there's so much magic in the making that you can materialize a crown!

What Turns You On

You adore a man who looks deep into your eyes and makes both you and time disappear. While you are a very sensual girl, what captivates you first is how someone affects your imagination.

Your favorite fantasy figure is the man who is destined by fate to be your soul mate or someone larger-than-life and terribly famous. Once your mind is transported and you're seeing yourself projected on a very large cinematic screen, your body kicks in. The actual play by play of the encounter is never quite as important as the fantasy-like quality of the overall picture. And there is no doubt about it, *that* has to excite you!

What Turns You Off

Men who are weak or obviously needy are the first to become instantly invisible. Men who are terribly unromantic and don't do anything to make you feel like a magical princess will be quickly put to the side, as will those who are crude, the ones who can't properly handle themselves, or who look like their mothers dressed them.

Your Cosmic Compatibility Guide

Note: This shows you how someone with your sun sign is most likely to get along with someone with his sun sign. Some combinations are instant chemistry; some are more challenging and require work and patience on both your parts. Keep in mind that this is based only on the sun sign. There are ten planets in all, and in a complete horoscope they are all important influences that affect the life of the relationship.

Aries: During the first few hours it might seem that the heavens have finally sent you a hero—the one you've been praying for since you were five. But alas, dear girl, this fellow moves on his own track, and it's likely that you just happened to be in his path. Dynamic, yes, but also self-centered, and he will leave you out in the cold during afterglow. He is hot in the *throes*, but that's not feeling to him. It's purely adventure. The minute his toes touch the floor he can be completely impersonal. He's probably thinking of the evening hockey game. Do yourself a favor and don't sit by the phone.

Taurus: He can't begin to *get* your sensitivity and stubbornly says that psychic stuff is hogwash. You think him the thickest of dullards. He doesn't even have a *spec* of curiosity! He thinks you're very charming and pretty but honestly indicates that what you *say* has no value. Mr. Taurus isn't mean, he's just a little dense and doesn't mind it. As a matter of fact, it works just right for *him*. But you're someone else entirely. Give yourself a break, for heaven's sake. How much do you *need* a boyfriend?

Gemini: The twin will intrigue you. He'll entertain you too. You both share a sense of humor that can be delightfully zany. However, he is in his head, while you are a creature of feeling. And while you are at home lounging on your chaise, remembering the romantic touches of your last rendezvous, this roué will be out with some blond, giggling and laughing anew. Mr. Gemini could break your heart if you open yourself too far. Watch it!

Cancer: An intuitive pathway exists between your souls. The crab can be trustworthy and caring. However, he can get completely caught up in meaningless little routines that you find absolutely *deadening*. Really, you don't want to hear about his boring problems at the office or why he wants to stay in for a cozy night of TV. You're going to have to bring him out of himself before you can be who you are around him. Don't give in to all his constrictions, Neptune girl. *Challenge* him and make him see life anew!

Leo: He plays to the ethereal romantic in you—with all the right props! You both have a child-like sense of magic that makes you special people. And as a couple you are special *together*. Now this is your hero on a white horse. Your belief in him will make miracles. His joy in you will bring out all your light. Together you will make oodles and oodles of romance and excitement—and simply blot out everything boring in the world!

Virgo: He is so cool, cerebral, and grounded in all the things you want to avoid. Consequently, he will annoy you more than a blight of adult acne. He has no imagination, no curiosity about anything but computers, and his favorite color is brown. Just being with him makes you feel like you're locked in a shabby office in a very small town. I don't think this one has hope.

Libra: Now this is a fellow who will tinker gracefully with your fantasies. You see he's quite an old-fashioned romantic too. He's in love with love—and *guess what*—so are you! He loves beauty—and so do you! He likes everything to be like a movie—and so do you! The difference is that he is much more cerebral, while you are emotional; still, he *will* cater to your moods. On those days when you feel inexplicably weepy, he'll bring you tulips and talk you into smiling. What could be better?

Scorpio: He is cold, hard, ruthless, and plays his cards close to his chest. Even getting him to tell you where he is going to the movies is a feat. Mr. Scorpio is compulsively secretive, tricky, manipulative, and, often by omission but sometimes by design, unkind. Your soft, poetic, spiritual side will never feel comfortable with this barracuda. All he wants to do is win. All *you* want is to feel more alive. Beware! He could bury you.

Sagittarius: This winsome fellow is a wonderful match for your love of magic and adventure. You share a sense of humor, a belief in the great beyond, and a spontaneity that makes everything exciting. He will respect where you're coming from and take you to lots of new places. This connection is about infinite possibilities and, potentially, never-ending love.

Capricorn: He is like a rich daddy who gives you an allowance and tells you what you to do with it. Yes, he may be a bastion of rock-solid support on your frail, confused days, but he is also grounded and entrenched in every facet of this world that you want to escape from. After awhile you want to escape from him as well! He has nothing to say that interests you, and when you open your mouth, he lets you know *he's* not even listening because *he* wants to talk.

Aquarius: You find all his fascinations fascinating. For a while, he is fun to talk to. However, he is cold and detached, while you are a myriad of emotions. He could never give you the support you need, especially on those needy days when everything seems chaotic. He is sorely lacking in both sympathy and affection. Lost in his head, he is more interested in laser printers than in deep human contact and just can't bridge the gap between head and heart.

Pisces: Now here is your soul mate who makes time stand still! Without speaking, you each know what the other is thinking and feeling. You look into each other's beautiful eyes and disappear into a world of your own making. Yes! Yes! Yes!

MOST MARVELOUS
COSMIC MATCHES

Pisces February 20–March 20
Libra September 24–October 23
Leo July 24–August 23

MOST DIFFICULT
COSMIC MATCHES

Virgo August 24–September 23
Aries March 21–April 20
Capricorn December 22–January 20

conclusion

So, dear girls, now you have all the insights you need to understand *the most important* aspects of yourself and *him*. I have told you all the luscious little secrets that will keep him guessing but keep you informed—all the things that are there but tough to see on the first date or in the first few months! Make THE BEDSIDE ASTROL-OGER COMPANION your bible. Put it under your pillow and have sweet dreams of the one you'll love!

Look for These Other Books From

COSMOPOLITAN®

THE NICE GIRL'S GUIDE TO SENSATIONAL SEX
by Nancy Kalish

Overcome your inhibitions and enjoy the fantastically ful-
filling lovemaking you've always dreamed about.

77229-9/$4.99 US/$5.99 Can

And at special introductory prices

THE BEDSIDE ASTROLOGER COMPANION
by Francesca Stuart

This companion to *Cosmopolitan*'s BEDSIDE
ASTROLOGER contains everything a Cosmo girl needs to
know about herself.

78070-4/$2.99 US/$3.99 Can

IRMA KURTZ'S ULTIMATE PROBLEM SOLVER
by Irma Kurtz

Cosmopolitan's celebrated problem-solver helps readers
untangle some of life's most complicated predicaments.

77977-3/$2.99 US/$3.99 Can